"And lovely are the rare days when the moor lies

sheeted with snow, and every spray is set with diamonds."

from *The New Forest*,
Elizabeth Godfrey, 1912

Contents

The Ghostly
Monks of Beaulieu

Stories of ghosts and supernatural happenings at Beaulieu Abbey abound. The Abbey was built for the Cistercian Monks in 1204 at the behest of King John. Beaulieu also received its name from John – 'Bellus Locus' meaning 'a fair place'. On the 10,000 acre Manor of Beaulieu stands the Palace House, the world famous Motor Museum and the ruins of the Abbey which was dissolved by Henry VIII in 1538.

Arthur Conan Doyle, creator of Sherlock Holmes, had a home in the New Forest – Bignell Wood at Brook, and he is buried in Minstead churchyard. He wrote an historical novel, *The White Company*, in 1891 which features the white-robed brothers of the Cistercian order at Beaulieu. His book begins:

> *The great bell of Beaulieu was ringing. Far away through the forest might be heard its musical clangour and swell.*

Conan Doyle, always fascinated with the supernatural, was mesmerised by the spell of Beaulieu Abbey and he is not alone. For centuries stories of apparitions, mostly of monks walking through the cloisters, have been passed down from generation to generation. Other phenomena such as the smell of incense and the sound of a choir singing late at night are recorded. Ghosts are seen even in broad daylight, but none of the sightings are sinister. The spirits seem perfectly at peace in their surroundings despite the thousands of visitors that come to Beaulieu every year.

In the early 1900s the vicar of the Abbey Church, which was once the refectory of the Abbey, was the Reverend Robert Powles. Powles, appearing perfectly sane in all other respects, was said to be on 'good terms' with his ghostly parishioners. He would hold a special midnight mass for the monks to attend on Christmas Eve; not, as you might think, in order to lay their souls to rest, but to welcome them as members of his congregation.

The sacred tapers' lights are gone
Grey moss has clad the altar stone,
The holy image is o'erthrown,
The bell has ceased to toll;
The long-ribbed aisles are burst and shrunk,
The holy shrine's to ruin sunk,
Departed is the pious monk;
God's blessing on his soul!

Beaulieu Abbey Ruins,
from *The New Forest Handbook*, 1876

New Forest
Mummers

The folk tradition of mumming was popular all over Britain until the First World War. Only a handful of mummers continued after the war but in recent years 'gangs' or 'sides' have been reforming to revive this festive tradition, which pre-dates Christianity. At one time most Forest villages would see a band of roving players, dressed in rag costume called 'tatters', celebrating the death of the old year and its rebirth as the new year. The plays follow a pattern and usually consist of a duel between an infidel Turkish knight and Saint George, during which one of them is killed, but later miraculously revived by a Doctor. All is overseen by Old Father Christmas and sometimes, old folk history favourites such as Johnny Jack, the Devil or Old King Cole. The identity of the players is concealed beneath tall hats and streamers, because superstition attached elements of magic to the performance and it was considered unlucky to name the mummers. Performers were mostly local farmers, villagers and tradesmen who often, under their cloak of anonymity, voiced political misgivings at the ever-present hardships experienced by the labouring classes.

The following play was adapted from The East Boldre Mummers Play which was performed at the Royal Oak, Hill Top, Beaulieu at Christmas, 1924 and is now enacted by the New Forest Mummers. St George has become King George and the infidel knight is the 'Turkey Snipe'.

Father Christmas:

In comes I, Old Father Christmas, welcome or a welcome not, I hope old Father Christmas never shall be forgot – the master of this house, I hope he is within, if he is pray tell us so and we shall then begin – for we have come this Christmas time a-purpose to be merry – so step in King George thou noble art, and let these good folk see thee play thy part.

King George:

In comes I, King George, from good old England sprung, my famous name throughout the world hath rung – indeed I am a man of courage bold, and with my sword I won ten crowns of gold.

'Twas me that fought the fiery dragon, and brought him to the slaughter, and by that means I wooed and won the King of Egypt's daughter – let any arrant knave defy King George so true and just, and a lusty blow from my brave sword will make him bite the dust.

Turkey Snipe:

Go to – boast not so loud King George, lest thy pride should have a fall – for lo there stands before you the bravest warrior of them all.

King George:

Who art thou to speak so rashly to King George?

Turkey Snipe:

In comes I a valiant Turkey Snipe, from far across the seas I come to fight, to fight and conquer thee King George the bold.

King George:

Wilt thou indeed?

Turkey Snipe:

Aye that I will – for I have sworn to drag thee down King George, usurp thy mighty kingdom and wear thy golden crown.

King George:

Waste no more words thou bragging Turkey Snipe, but draw forth thy sword if thou be not a coward, and fight.

A Duel ensues – the Turkey Snipe is slain.

Second Turk:

What hast thou done King George, what hast thou done – behold my brother lies a-bleeding on the ground – his life is ebbing like the setting sun, what hast thou done King George, what hast thou done?

King George:

Question me not thou prating knave, yon Turkey Snipe was by me vanquished in fair fight – he would have usurped my kingdom and my crown if I had not so bravely cut him down.

Second Turk:

Is there no where a Doctor to be found – to heal my brother of his grievous wound?

Doctor:

Yes indeed there be a Doctor nigh – in comes I old Doctor Brown, the best and cleverest in the town, what carries medicines and pills to cure all ills.

Second Turk:

Can'st thou then ease my brother's fearful pain?

Doctor:

Aye that can I, and what's more, if he be dead I'll bring him back to life again.

Second Turk:

What fee do'st thou ask good Doctor for carrying out thy noble task?

Doctor:

Ten golden guineas is my fee, but if thou be a poor man, I'll rest content with three.

Second Turk:

Nay, nay, wealthy Snipes from Turkey land we be, and so in full will I pay thy fee – here hold out thy hand.

Doctor:

Thank ye kind sir – and now to tend thy brother's fearful wound – from which I fear he has already swooned – or is he dead?

Second Turk:

Oh, say not so!

Doctor:

I fear he is – but take heart good sir, for I have here a life restoring elixir – lo, to the dead man's lips I puts this bottle, and pours the contents down his throttle – see, he that was dead now rises, thy brother lives I say!

Second Turk:

Oh wondrous sight – he will return to fight King George another day.

King George:

Yea, another day, but not now, for 'tis the season of goodwill, when men of peace should eat and drink their fill, so sheath thy swords and shake my hand, let mirth and laughter echo through the land.

Father Christmas:

And so say I, let everyone here be of good cheer, for Christmas comes but once a year – hurrah! for roast beef, plum pudding and beer.

King George:

Now the good master knows we're here we'll want for nothing, never fear.

Turkey Snipe:

A proper gentleman he be, who'll welcome us right royally.

Father Christmas:

But stay – who might yon stranger be who comes this way?

Little Johnny Jack:

In comes I, Little Johnny Jack, my wife and family all on my back – my family's large and my wife is small, and poor Little Johnny's got to feed them all – so come good masters, give us a treat, a slice of roast beef and some mince pies to eat, and a mug of old ale seein' 'tis Christmas time, we'll make us all merry and so ends my rhyme.

Father Christmas:

Ladies and Gentlemen, if you've enjoyed our play – please don't send us poor mummers empty handed away – for a few ha-pennies and pennies will buy us some beer – so we wish you a Merry Christmas and a Happy New Year!

The present day New Forest Mummers group was founded by David Williams of Marchwood and they have been performing regularly since 1967. They travel round the streets and pubs of the New Forest, mostly on Boxing Day. The money raised at their performances goes to a charity, often locally based. A few of the past beneficiaries have been the Fenwick Hospital, Lyndhurst, Ashurst Hospital League of Friends, Totton Dialysis Appeal and Wessex Cancer Trust.

New Forest Mummers outside the Balmer Lawn Hotel, 1983.

Rose C. De Crespigny and Horace Hutchinson explore the theme of mummers in their book *The New Forest: its Traditions, Inhabitants and Customs*, published in 1895.

... the mummers still go about at Christmas-tide, though their profession is degenerating. There is still one band of mummers, worthy of the name, which performs scraps from what were once mystery or morality plays; but it has become the habit for youths to dress up and pose as the real mummers, though they have no ideas beyond a few topical songs. The real old mummers will doubtless soon disappear into the limbo whither other real old things have preceded them. The eternal fitness of things appears not always present to the forester's mind, for lately a boy came to a house in the Forest on Christmas Eve, with blackened face, white-painted mouth, and on his head an old tall hat which had a peacock's feather stuck in it, but no brim. In this singularly appropriate disguise, he began singing, with pious fervour, 'Whilst shepherds watched their flocks by night.' His was, at all events, no intentional irreverence, and his general cheeriness suited the festal occasion.

St Nicholas Church, Brockenhurst

St Nicholas Church at Brockenhurst is the oldest church in the New Forest, being mentioned in Domesday. The church is set on top of a hill, a quarter of a mile south east of the level crossing. There is speculation as to whether the site may date back to pagan times and the existing church shows evidence of late Norman architecture in the South Doorway and Saxon 'herring-bone' masonry in the walls. Inside, the bowl of the font, lead-lined and fashioned from Purbeck Stone, dates from the twelfth century.

St Nicholas Church, Brockenhurst, from a watercolour by Barry Peckham

In the churchyard the Great Yew Tree, which stands at the west end of the church, is possibly as old as the church, since its girth in 1793 was already 15 feet! On the east side of the cemetery, near the memorial stone to the one hundred New Zealand and Indian soldiers who died in hospitals at Brockenhurst during the First World War, is the sculptured head-stone to 'Brusher' Mills, the famous snake-catcher. Brusher is said to have gained his nickname from brushing clean the wickets of local cricket grounds and also, one hard winter, when he daily brushed the ice for skaters on the lake in Foxlease Park.

The dedication of the parish church of Brockenhurst seems shrouded in mystery. *The Victoria County History* (Vol 4), published in 1911, firmly states that the church's dedication is unknown. Most guide books and literary works on the New Forest also stated that the dedication was unknown, calling St Nicholas simply, the parish church. Elizabeth Croly seems to have found the answer when she published her book *The Lure of the New Forest* in 1925. She says that for hundreds of years people disputed about the dedication of the church, and 'none knew what saint had it under his protection. In recent years, however, there turned up in Winchester the will of John Draper, 1539, containing this clause: *I bequeath to the Church of Saynt Nicholas in Brockenhurst 1 heyferr*. That heifer settled the matter,' says Elizabeth Croly and certainly there seems no doubt in the minds of people today.

St Nicholas is the patron saint of children and scholars. In England his feast day, 6 December, was celebrated with great solemnity in ancient times, with someone dressing as a bishop and distributing gifts and sweets to the 'good children'. Santa Claus is a corruption of the name and is now associated specifically with Christmas. The present custom of putting toys in a stocking late on Christmas Eve, while the children are asleep, and the legend of Santa Claus travelling around in a sleigh pulled by reindeer, was introduced into England from Germany about 1840. Another influence came from America where the old Dutch settlers of New York kept a San Claus holiday.

Toys, Toys, Toys

For many children Christmas would not be complete without a toy, and simple wooden toys have delighted children through the generations. Brockenhurst and Burley were the centres for the New Forest wooden toy industry, before the Second World War. Elizabeth Godfrey in her book on the New Forest in 1912, visits Brockenhurst.

Hard by the station, on a bare plot of ground, once a small village green, stands the smithy at the meeting of the ways... Just beyond the forge a low-browed workshop and thatched cottage used to stand a little back from the road, where Mr Pope and his forebears for many generations – one may say for many centuries – practised a unique industry, the making of hobby horses, for which the district has been famed time out of mind. The little old premises with precious store of wood were burnt in a disastrous fire one Christmas night; but the old business is still carried on, though in new quarters, and still the traveller may see in the station yard piles upon piles of these conventional steeds of exactly the same pattern, beloved of our ancestors in their childhood, straight-bodied, straight-legged, standing on four little wheels, so as to be dragged along by a string, each adorned with a narrow strip of fur nailed along his neck to represent a mane, and brightened with daubs of red and blue paint, laid on with just the traditional touch. They go forth in their hundreds – north, south, east and west – to find a market; so children must love them still, and have not grown too sophisticated to find joy in their crude suggestion.

Brockenhurst was also the base for Whittington's New Forest Toys factory in the years between the two world wars. Frank Whittington and his wife, the painter and commercial artist Marjorie Hood, came to Brockenhurst after the Great War and set up a business producing hand carved wooden toys. By 1922 the toys were so popular that the Whittington's opened a small factory which eventually employed sixteen men and women. As well as New Forest animals, Whittington's specialised in Noah's Arks, farm yard figures and stagecoaches and they were bought by Harrods, Selfridges and other major London stores. Frank Whittington was a devout Christian and served as a church-warden for St Saviours, Brockenhurst. He carved nativity sets for several churches in the area, including St Saviours, and some are still used at Christmas.

Burleytoys, the brainchild of Colonel Mumby and C. T. Eaton, began in the small workshop at the rear of Colonel Mumby's garage in Burley. They specialised in 'action' toys – the 'Buster' fort which exploded when hit by a direct shot, battleships and submarines which 'blew up' and dolls' houses which could be dismantled and packed away. They soon had to move to larger premises and employed a staff of around thirty people at their height. Their main outlet in London was Gamages and great numbers of toys were exported to America. Burleytoys are now much sought after by toy collectors. Both businesses ceased at the outbreak of the Second World War because of difficulties in staffing and obtaining supplies.

Traditional Recipes from a Forest Cabin

I rene Soper lives at Abbots Well near Fordingbridge, deep in the heart of the New Forest. Juliette de Baïracli Levy lived at Abbots Well when she wrote *Wanderers in the New Forest*, and Irene has followed her example and become the author of several books. *New Forest Cookery* was first published in 1983 and is much more than a book of recipes. In it she weaves the story of cottager, farmer, commoner and gypsy, giving insights into their way of life both past and present. Irene spent twelve years collecting the recipes some of which are very old and

Bringing in the Boar's Head at Christmas

have been passed down the generations by word of mouth only. Others were found on dusty scraps of paper at the back of cupboards. All are authentic local dishes. She even includes, for its historic value, a recipe for boar's head which was found in a farmhouse on the estate of one of the last of the Forest manors to the north west that was held by William the Conqueror.

Here are some extracts from *New Forest Cookery*.

Chestnuts are the most versatile of nuts lending themselves to a variety of uses in cooking. The old traditional way of roasting them in the glowing embers is still my favourite way of eating them but here is a recipe which makes a very good stuffing for the turkey.

Chestnut Stuffing

One pound of chestnuts, half a pint of stock, one ounce of butter, grated rind of one lemon, one tea-spoonful of sugar, quarter of a pound of bread-crumbs, quarter of a pound of ham or bacon, one dessertspoonful of parsley, one egg and seasoning.

Remove the outside shell from the nuts, then blanch them and remove the inner skin. Stew the nuts in stock or water until they are quite tender and dry. Then pound them to a paste with the ham or bacon finely chopped. Add all the other ingredients, moistening with beaten egg or a little milk.

In winter, with a log fire in the cabin, we sometimes have girdle scones for tea. A girdle (sometimes called a griddle) is a round piece of thick iron hanging on a chain and heated over an open fire. It can also be used on a range or stove. You can use a grill burner for this recipe or a griddle if you have one. The griddle should be well heated whilst preparing the dough. Before cooking, it can be either greased or sprinkled with flour. Afterwards, the girdle should never be washed. Clean it by rubbing with coarse salt and a piece of paper, then give it a final dust. Our girdle was given to us by the Forest naturalist, Eric Ashby. It came from 'Badger Cottage' where it was regularly used by his mother to make these delicious scones.

Badger Cottage Girdle Scones

One pound of flour, half a teaspoonful cream of tartar, one teaspoonful carbonate of soda, a little salt, and sour milk.

Sieve all the dry ingredients into a basin and make a well in the centre. Add enough milk to make a light dough, turn out on a floured board, and divide into four. Then take one piece at a time and flatten it into a round scone, about half an inch thick. Cut in four again and place the scones on a hot greased girdle. Cook about five minutes on either side. The scones should be nicely browned on both sides, and they are ready when the edges are dry. Serve with butter. A few currants may be added if liked.

November the twenty-sixth really sees the start of the preparations for Christmas in the New Forest. For that is the traditional date on which the gypsies are allowed to start picking the holly to sell at the local markets and to make wreaths. Already they have filled their sacks with moss gathered from the boggy paths on the side of the hill above Abbots Well. This moss is used in the foundations of the wreaths. One old gypsy lady living in the village can always be seen at that time of year colourfully dressed in a long skirt, short coat with flowered apron and headscarf, pushing a pram overflowing with holly towards the town.

Our small local Forest town Fordingbridge is a throng of activity as the festive season progresses. Outside the butcher's shop hang rows of hares, pheasants and turkeys. Lighted Christmas trees shine above every shop and in the square people gather to sing traditional carols around a bigger lit tree. Back in the village the carol singers find their way along the dark lanes by the light of a lantern on a long pole. At one time carol singers on Christmas Eve were given a warming spiced drink. The Christmas Wassail Bowl was usually composed of strong ale, the froth of roasted apples, cloves and cinnamon, and a grate of nutmeg, ginger, and brown sugar.

Through the open doorway of the village church comes the sound of more carols sung this time to the accompaniment of the local silver band. Approaching the church, our pathway is gilded by the glowing colours of the stained glass window.

Inside, a huge Christmas tree stands shining with coloured lights and cascades of gold and silver tinsel. Every seat is filled, and after the service coffee and sandwiches are served in the adjacent hall where everyone can meet and discuss the coming festive season.

On Christmas Eve the kitchen is a very busy place. Although the cake and puddings have been made for weeks there are still the mince-pies to make, the chestnut stuffing to mix, vegetables to prepare, the trifle to make, and the cake to decorate.

Christmas Cake

Ten ounces of plain flour, pinch of salt, one level teaspoonful of mixed spice, half a level teaspoonful of grated nutmeg, four ounces of glacé cherries, twelve ounces of seedless raisins, twelve ounces of sultanas, eight ounces of currants, eight ounces of butter, eight ounces of soft brown sugar, four eggs, two tablespoonfuls of sherry, two ounces of whole almonds, one ounce of crystallized ginger, one heaped teaspoonful of grated lemon rind, two ounces of mixed peel, chopped.

Grease a round eight-inch deep cake tin. Line with two layers of greased greaseproof paper. Tie a double band of brown paper round the outside of the tin. Pre-heat oven to 350°F and reduce to 300°F after fifteen minutes. Sift flour, salt, spice and nutmeg into a bowl. Wash and dry the cherries. Chop fairly finely. Clean the raisins, sultanas and currants by putting them in a sieve with a little extra flour. Rub well until all the flour falls through the sieve, discard flour. Cream butter and brown sugar in a bowl until smooth and fluffy. Beat eggs together in a basin. Gradually beat eggs into the creamed mixture. Stir in the sherry. Put almonds into a small pan of water and bring to the boil. Drain and skin. Cut the nuts finely. Chop the ginger. Stir together ginger, almonds, cleaned fruit, cherries, lemon rind and peel. Stir fruit and nuts mixture into sifted flour, and gradually fold into creamed mixture. Put into prepared tin, smooth the top and make a well in centre. Cook on lower shelf of the oven for four hours. When cake is quite cold, and it should be left to cool for twelve hours, wrap in a clean cloth, then in greaseproof paper, until ready to ice.

Christmas at Nowelhurst

R. D. Blackmore is best known for his romance of Exmoor, *Lorna Doone*, but he wrote fourteen other novels, including *Cradock Nowell: A Tale of the New Forest*, in 1866. The eponymous hero, Cradock Nowell is heir to ancient Nowelhurst Hall, based on Burley Lodge.

From a rising ground the house has sweet view of all the forest changes, and has seen three hundred springs wake in glory, and three hundred autumns waning. Spreading away from it wider, wider, slopes 'the Chase', as they call it, with great trees stretching paternal arms in the vain attempt to hold it. For two months of the twelve, when the heather is in blossom, all that chase is a glowing reach of amaranth and purple. Then it fades away to pale orange, dim olive, and a rusty brown when Christmas shudders over it...

Blackmore weaves the tale of Cradock Nowell's love for Amy, the daughter of the parson, John Rosedew. Many vicissitudes must be overcome, of course, before the course of true love

can run smooth. To modern tastes Blackmore's prose may appear florid and ponderous but he evokes a scene and mood and the Forest backdrop is used to good effect. Eöa is Cradock's cousin; half-Afghanistani, she was brought up amongst a robber tribe in the Himalayas and is still learning the niceties of English gentry life.

Upon the Christmas morning, the parish flocked to church; and the church was dressed so beautifully that the parish was amazed. Amy and Eöa had made the wreaths, the garlands, and rosettes; there was only one cross to be discovered - a badly-bred Maltese one. Eöa had been walking over the barbarous pew-screens (like the travisses in a stable), springing from one to another, with a cable of flowers and evergreens, as easily and calmly as she would step from the scraper to the door-mat. Of course she had never heard of that sort of thing before, but she took to it at once, as she did to any thing pretty; and soon she was Amy's mistress, as indeed she must be every one's, unless she could not bear them.

The sons of the Forest looked up with amazement as they shambled in one after another, and an old woodcutter went home for his axe, lest the ivy should throttle the pillars.

The Old Road
A Tale of the New Forest

BY DESMOND A. LEPARD

It is said that civilisation is only a thin veneer,
And just a crack in the surface can uncover a well of fear,
A morass of superstition, where reason is put to rout,
And comfortable, clear convictions degenerate into doubt.

Four of us boarded the local stage at the *Angel*, in Lymington town,
With Coachman John that made five souls, all of us Ringwood bound,
And the cheerful clatter and bustle as the coach prepared to leave,
Was enriched by a note of revelry, for was this not New Year's Eve?

In the year of our Lord 1815, a time of England's might,
When Wellington, at Waterloo, had shown how Englishmen fight,
And healed, with that great victory, the nation's running sore,
By bringing peace to the people, after weary years of war.

No Christmastide had ever seen more wassail and goodwill,
And the poorest in the parishes for once had fed their fill,
For the Mayor himself had made it known that joy should come to all,
And even the Frenchy prisoners had danced at the Yuletide Ball.

But that day we four good citizens, merchants of some renown,
Were travelling to Ringwood, to dine that night at the Crown,

Meanwhile, to keep out the bitter cold, we had cracked a bottle or two,
While Coachman John had supped right well on the Angel's famed home brew.

'Come, gentleman all,' called Coachman John, ''tis time for us to go,
The wind has turned, it's due nor'east, and I don't doubt it will snow.'
We hurried then, though we were loth to leave the fireside bright,
For we were aware that the Forest was no place to be snowbound at night.

Though John had a brace of pistols and each of us wore a sword
And none of us was a coward, yet we knew there roamed abroad
Desperate and dangerous rogues, vagabonds, thieves – and worse,
Who would slit the throat of an honest man for the guineas in his purse.

The wind, as we hastened across the yard, was razor-sharp and raw,
And its icy fingers froze the flesh through the thick cloth coats we wore.
The coach-springs squeaked as we climbed aboard and huddled in our seats,
With blankets wrapped around us and hot bricks at hand and feet.

John swiftly mounted the driving-box, felt the bite of the wind, and swore,
Then grinned at a buxom serving wench, 'You'd keep me warm, for sure!'
The ostlers let go the horses' heads and the coach, with a jolt and a lurch,
Moved forward through the *Angel* arch and swung right towards the church.

Through the town we drove at spanking pace and soon we could espy
The high, bare mounds of Buckland Rings, stark against the sky,
While lower down the great reed beds stood drowning in the flood
Which well-nigh every winter makes our water-meadows mud.

I looked at my companions, men I'd known all my life,
The Manson brothers, Paul and Hugh, whose sister was my wife,
And whose good Forest timber, oaken planking from their yard,
Was part of every man-o'-war launched at Bucklers Hard.

Beside me, Martin Johnson, late of the Fusiliers,
Who had gallantly campaigned, unscathed, for nearly fifteen years,
'Til the sabre of a French hussar, south of Salamanca,

Had sent him home and changed his rank, from brigadier to banker.

But the wine we'd drunk in our merry mood was strong, and talk soon lagged,
And eyelids drooped as the coach rolled on, and on four chests four chins sagged,
And none of us noticed the first snowflakes, soft and white as they swirled,
For as John pulled out onto Setley Plain we were sleeping, and dead to the world.

How long I slept I cannot say - I awoke with a violent start,
And the certainty that something was wrong, and a pounding in my heart,
While all around was a curious light, a strangely luminous glow,
Which revealed my three companions and, dim through the window, snow.

Martin Johnson and the Mansons lay sprawled out, still fast asleep,
And it seemed to me uncanny that their slumber should be so deep
For surely what had awakened me should have aroused them, too,
And I shouted out as I shook each one, 'Wake up, Martin, Paul, Hugh!'

There was no response, I thought they were dead – then I saw, thank God, I was wrong,
By the regular movement of each man's chest as he breathed steady and strong,
But their features were still and lifeless, as though carved out of stone,
And I knew that whatever lay ahead I would have to face alone.

I climbed from the coach into a world snowbound, silent and still,
The weird light illumined all, and I recognised Wilverley Hill,
Across the valley Wootton sloped, and I knew, though I peered in vain,
That far ahead the turnpike ran, in the shadow of Goatspen Plain.

As a boy I'd explored this countryside on my Forest pony's back,
I'd forded the streams and skirted the bogs and climbed every hill and track,
I'd known where the otter took his trout, and the honey buzzard flew,
I'd seen badger cubs playing by moonlight and followed the fox through the dew.

I'd walked in the deep inclosures by the charcoal-burner's hut,
And, on quiet October evenings, heard the red deer roar at rut,
I'd skated over Hatchett Pond, and laughed as the summer rain
Spangled the hair of the gipsy maid who I'd kissed on Red Shoot Plain.

I'd welcomed the wild December gales when they raged in from the sea,
And watched the great oaks writhe and twist and bow to their mastery,
I loved this Forest in all its moods, and I'd learned its secret ways,
And it had been playground and schoolroom since my earliest childhood days.

But the Forest this night, as I stood alone, was an awful, alien place,
With features entirely familiar – but wearing no friendly face,
But breathing a brooding menace, an evil, malignant air,
And I felt a numbing helplessness, like a rabbit in a snare.

I looked up at Coachman John, that big man, bluff and brave,
And I saw how he sat on the driving-box, like a statue over a grave,
Shoulders hunched in caped top-coat, tricorne rammed low on his head,
While his thick-gloved hands held the reins to horses as still as the dead.

Frightened, alone, in that frozen world, above all I craved human speech,
When the silence was violently shattered, ripped apart by an eldritch screech
Shocked, I staggered against the coach while beneath my feet the ground
Shook and trembled and rumbled – then again that unearthly sound.

I saw a huge black form rush by, belching fire and smoke,
The stench was foul and sulphurous and I thought that I would choke,
But though I smelt its acrid breath, I even then knew well
That this was not some demon, or a fiery hound from Hell.

No pale apparition this, sad fruit of an unhinged mind,
But something hard and tangible which was drawing close behind
Several great wheeled boxes, each one filled with light,
All thundering by in line, almost snakelike in the night.

Then it had gone, and I stood once more, alone in the silence again,
But sharp and sure were the details of the picture burned in my brain,
For, in the boxes as they had passed, like cattle confined in a pen,
During just one fleeting moment I know that I saw men.

With senses reeling I half fell, my body could stand no more,

And stumbling to the coach I clambered back in through the door,
I was drained of any courage, trembling weakly, and I wept,
I collapsed back in my seat, closed my aching eyes, and slept.

Then I heard Martin's laughter and saw him pretend to frown,
'Come, wake up, you old rogue, we are nearing Ringwood town!
And tell us, pray, what was your dream while you slumbered long and deep?
For you have kept us all awake, muttering in your sleep!'

But how could I answer his question? And who, indeed, would believe
Such an unlikely tale – especially on New Year's Eve?
But I know something happened out there in that curious light,
And I see it all as clear today as I did on that far-off night.

I've since made that journey many times, and always I tense in my seat
As we reach the place, and I live it again, and feel my heart miss a beat,
And you ask why a sensible man like me still trembles with foolish fear?
Well, they say commonsense, like civilisation, is only a thin veneer!

Historical footnote: The Southampton and Dorchester Railway (long defunct) opened in 1847, some thirty years after the above events occurred, and the track across the New Forest is believed by some to have followed part of the old Lymington to Ringwood stagecoach road.

Christmas Oaks

BY RICHARD REEVES

There are a great number of named trees in the New Forest, the most famous being the Knightwood Oak, followed by the Twelve Apostles at Burley Lodge. Most of the named trees were so named because their massive size made them focal points, while others commemorated an event. An example of this is the Eagle Oak, in Knightwood Inclosure, where, John Wise states, the last Fish Eagle was shot by a Forest Keeper early in the 1800s. I wonder how many other species were eliminated!

In a different class was the Cadenham Oak, near Cadnam, which was said to come into leaf on old Christmas Day (5 January). Mention is made of this tree by William Gilpin who, one year, had Michael Lawrence, landlord of the White Hart Inn, send him some of the freshly unsheaved leaves as soon as they were available. He received them on 5 January 1782. Gilpin sent an account to the *Salisbury Journal* for 10 January 1786 which reports that the leaves that year had first been found on 3 January. According to Horace Hutchinson the tree died early in the nineteenth century and a successor was named the Cadenham Oak although it did not have the same early leafing peculiarities.

Interestingly Gilpin writes in his book of 1791 that the original tree was 'a tall straight plant of no great age, and apparently vigorous,' so why it should have died early the next century is a mystery although Gilpin did mention that 'its top had been injured'.

Hutchinson also tells of the tradition of the 'Rufus Oak'. This tree supposedly deflected the arrow that killed King William II (Rufus) and also came into leaf in mid-winter. This seems to have first been recorded by Leland writing in the 1530s and '40s, so it was obviously an old tale. By 1745 this tree had died and John, Lord Delaware, of Bolderwood Lodge, replaced it's remains with the Rufus Stone which, in turn, was replaced by the present iron casing.

John Aubrey writing in the late 1600s in his *Monumenta Brittanica*, a book finished in 1693, mentions a winter-leafing oak at Castle Malwood. He states that:

On the north side, hard by is the Oake, that bears green Leaves, Budds, here and there among the principal branches upon Christmas; which I have seen: it is but a low Tree, dead top't, not very big, and rotten below: it hath been abused by Hacking, King Charles II hath paled it about.

Aubrey then goes on to relate the tradition of the killing of Rufus. In his *Natural History of Wiltshire*, Aubrey adds more detail. He seems to have written this piece before that quoted above as it seems when writing the following, he had not yet seen the oak:

...within the trenches of the Castle of Molwood ... is an old oake, which is a pollard and short. It putteth forth young leaves on Christmas day, for about a week at that time of the yeare. Old Mr Hastings, of Woodlands, was wont to send a basket full of them every yeare to King Charles I. ... Mr Perkins, who lives in the New Forest, sayes that there are two other oakes besides that which breed green buddes on Christmas day (pollards also), but not constantly. One is within two leagges of the King's-oake, the other a mile and a halfe off.

The 'Old Mr Hastings' is Henry Hastings of Woodlands in Dorset, who held the office of Master Keeper in the Bailiwick of Westlynwood until his death in 1650 at the age of ninety-nine years, though it has been claimed he was one hundred years of age at his death.

This Rufus Oak was also unlikely to have had anything to do with the killing of Rufus as such a tree would probably have died long before the eighteenth century. It was likely, however, that such a winter-leafing oak existed. A probable reference to this Rufus commemorating tree was given by the seventeenth century botanist, Dr William How, who annotated his personal *Phytologia Brittanica* with the following:

Quercus natalitis Dni virens, ye Christmas greene oake, ... neere ye Castle of Malwood, Hampshire, Kg. J. went to visit and caused it to be paled about.

Dr How had written *Phytologia Brittanica* in 1650, and he died in 1656, so presumably this Oak was still alive at that time. The 'Kg.J.' probably refers to King James I as it is unlikely that King John (reigned 1199-1216) would have visited this tree as it would, at best, have only been a sapling at the time of his visit. King James is a much more likely candidate. His reign certainly produced much documentation on the Royal Forests, and the tree would have been mature when he visited. The tradition of the Canterton Glen site is interesting. If you don't know where Rufus was killed, but want to commemorate the occasion, what better than to choose a tree which comes into leaf around Christmas time?

The statement that the tree was 'paled about', and that the name was given as the 'Christmas greene oake' connects it to another reference. Mention is made in the accounts of the Under Woodward, Francis Bennett, of payments made for paling in the 'Greene tree'. The accounts were for the two years up to 1620, which would tie in nicely to King James ordering the paling as his reign lasted over the period 1603-25. The total cost of the work was £2 19s 6d which was over twice the wages of the Forests' chief keepers. Obviously this was an important tree. The high capital expenditure can be explained if the two references relate to the same tree for it is hard to think of a tree more important than one commemorating the death of King William II, and paled about, under instruction from King James. Interestingly Hutchinson states that the Rufus Oak was empaled by King Charles II, which ties in with Aubrey's Oak at Castle Malwood. It also suggests that it had not before been fenced, though it is possible that this was a rebuilding of the old fence, or simply a failure to remember exactly which King had ordered the tree to be empaled. However, the tree empaled by King James I was near, and not at, Castle Malwood, which suggests this was a different tree though it does seem unlikely that two Stuart kings would empale two separate trees in the same area.

Gilpin states that he had been informed of another winter-leafing oak being found in the vicinity of the Rufus Stone and suggests that this may be a descendant of the Rufus Oak. This could certainly be true if the peculiarities are genetic, although such trees have often been found to have received a lightning strike, which may have reset the internal 'clock' of the tree. Whatever the truth about these trees they will continue to add fascination and tradition to the local scene.

And a fair stone in green Malwood
Informs the traveller where he stood,
The memorable tree.

W. S. Rose

The legend of the Cadnam, or Cadenham, Oak is well known to all Foresters. This version appeared in *The New Forest: its Traditions, Inhabitants and Customs* by Rose C. De Crespigny and Horace Hutchinson, in 1895.

There was a very famous oak at Cadnam, which was said by the natives to throw out buds each Christmas day. In truth there seems but little doubt that it did show signs of young shoots in the winter time, but that it was so exact to a day is scarcely to be credited. The legend goes that the monks, in olden time, forced on buds by artificial heat, and then persuaded a countryman – was it, perchance, by the medium of small bribes, or only of indulgences? – to stick these forced buds on to the tree. It is always thus – the explainers of miracles suggest explanations far more miraculous than the miracles explained. That a forester should have been deceived by the forced bud is too large a proposition for our credulity. It is much simpler to accept the original miracle without reserve. On the other hand this particular oak was struck down by lightning two or three years ago, which is unfortunate in two respects. In the first place it does not 'jump with' the theory that the tree was supernaturally cared for, and in the second it makes it impossible for us to test the miracle by experiment. Botanists, declining to receive the miracle, yet convinced that the tree sprouted in winter, have suggested that its forbears lived in a country whose spring-tide corresponded to our winter-tide, and that the Cadnam tree maintained its inherited instincts in spite of a change of climate. Thus black swans, in this country, sanguinely attempt nursery experiments at the date of the Australian spring. The cold and frost are not tempered to them, however, for all their pious faithfulness to their traditions. The buds of the Cadnam Oak were always frost-bitten, like those of the famous Glastonbury thorn, with which nature used to play a similar little practical joke.

W. H. Rogers *Guide to the New Forest*, which was published from 1878 to 1913, gives a description of where to find the possible successor to the original Cadnam Oak, explaining that 'in an old wood engraving of the Cadnam Oak, dated 1833, a young one is represented at its side'.

The tree is best seen from the main road to Southampton, and is about half-way between the Sir John Barleycorn Inn (a good sample of a country wayside inn) and a chapel inscribed 'Primitive Methodist Chapel, 1866'. It stands on a small piece of forest land on the north side of the road, close to the side or end of a cottage garden. It is a tree of somewhat tall appearance, of no very great age or dimensions. It is split and much rotted down the trunk, from where the branches spring, to the ground.

Christmas
School Treats

Compared with the luxury of a modern Christmas, most New Forest children in Victorian and Edwardian times experienced very frugal celebrations. Holly, mistletoe and paper lanterns would have been the extent of the decorations. For most cottagers Christmas day lunch would be a fat capon or roast beef and Christmas pudding washed down with home-made ale or wine. There would be little money to spare for presents; a home-made wooden toy with, perhaps, an orange and a few nuts would be the only contents of their stocking. If they were lucky their church or school, or the local gentry, would organize a Christmas party, with feasting, entertainment and gifts. Here are accounts of the Emery Down, Woodlands and Copythorne Children's Treats given in *The New Forest Magazine*, 1893. Christmas day had fallen on a Sunday, perhaps explaining the increase in the congregation.

Emery Down

Christmas Day

Our little church was again decorated with much simple taste and appropriateness for the Holy Festival of Christmas, and the congregations were good at all the services. The number of communicants was much greater than it had been for some years past.

The Children's Treat

On Tuesday, Jan. 10th, the little folks had their annual Christmas Treat, in the Schoolroom. After a capital tea, which they most thoroughly enjoyed, the Vicar took them round the world by the aid of the magic lantern and some very capital views, concluding with some merry pictures at which they laughed to their hearts content, and all went home very happy and laden with oranges, cake, and sweets or nuts.

Woodlands

On December 16th Mrs Mansfield gave a treat to the Infants attending the Woodlands Infant School. After tea the little ones received a number of presents, each child having besides a toy, a useful garment; scarlet cloaks or navy blue serge dresses for the little girls, and great coats or suits for the little boys.

Copythorne

Christmas Day

Our Church never looked prettier than it did this year; the white and red flowers sent from Paultons, and so tastefully arranged by Mrs Sanders, looked so well in contrast with the abundance of evergreen and holly berries. The services were well attended, and the offertory amounted to nearly £6. In the afternoon carols were sung as usual.

Christmas Treat

Mrs Maitland's Christmas tree at the Bartley Infant School was as popular as ever this year. The dolls in their pink, white, or blue had such a pretty effect, and there were other toys in abundance, as well as sweets, crackers, etc; to delight the hearts of the little folks. An excellent tea was provided to which ample justice was done, after which the children sang a pretty verse, wishing all their kind friends a Merry Christmas and a Happy New Year.

Christmas School Treat

Logs to Burn

'For pleasure a wood fire's the thing.' So said William Cobbett in his *Rural Rides*, and whilst some of Cobbett's views may be considered dubious, about fires he was not wrong. There is nothing quite like a log fire for imparting that special glow to a winter's evening. Wood makes a friendlier and more fragrant fire than coal and, if well made, is less work as wood ash does not need to be removed every morning. It makes a good bed for the new logs which light easily with a little kindling.

It is best to use four or five sturdy logs to start your fire, as too few will not burn well. Don't allow the fire to get too low and always place new logs at the back. Logs should be dry, and generally, well seasoned. Exceptions are holly and ash; an old saying goes 'Ash when green is fit for a queen.' No Forester worth his salt will use spruce for choice as it gives off sparks and tends to smoulder rather than burn. Birch tends to burn too fast and chestnut is too soft. Fruit trees of all kinds give off a delightful aroma. The best logs are ash, hawthorn, oak, beech, hornbeam, yew and acacia. The old rhyme 'Logs to burn' is a useful reminder.

Logs to burn, logs to burn,
Logs to save the coal a turn.
Here's a word to make you wise:
When you hear the woodman's cries,
Never heed his usual tale
That he has splendid logs for sale –
But read these lines and generally learn
The proper kind of logs to burn.
Oak logs will warm you well
If they're old and dry.
Large logs of pine woods smell,
But the sparks will fly.
Beech logs for Christmas time;

Yew logs heat well.
'Scotch' logs it is a crime
For anyone to sell.
Birch logs will burn too fast,
Chestnut scarce at all.
Hawthorn logs are good to last
If you cut them at the fall.
Holly logs will burn like wax,
You should burn them green.
Elm logs like smouldering flax,
No flame is to be seen.
Pear logs and apple logs,
They will scent your room.
Cherry logs across the dogs
Smell like flowers in bloom.
But Ash logs all smooth and grey,
Burn them green or old;
Buy up all that come your way,
They're worth their weight in gold.

The word yule is from the Old English gêol, the name given to a heathen festival at the winter solstice. The massive yule log was laid across the hearth with great ceremony on Christmas Eve and lit with a brand from the previous year's log. Oak and beech are the woods usually associated with the yule log. They are slow-burning and give out tremendous warmth. The oak in particular, will keep alight for days and nights, and this would have allowed the revellers low maintenance heating while they concentrated on the serious business of celebrating.

The Counterfeit Christmas Axe

BY PETER ROBERTS

Minstead has always been a funny place where people do things differently. Its position, surrounded on all sides by the woods, has meant that the inhabitants have for centuries relied on the Forest for their livelihood. Nicholas Cobb was from a village family that specialised in charcoal burning. He had not long married Mandlyn Johnson, whose father, Thomas and sister, Elizabeth lived close by the ford, when his new father-in-law died. His death meant the house had to be vacated. So Christmas, 1612, saw Nicholas helping his sister-in-law clear out her old family home prior to her moving in with him and Mandlyn.

Making sure that nothing had been forgotten he looked behind a rafter in the roof and found, buried in the thatch, an iron stamp. It was, in fact, a replica of the marking axe used by the Forest Woodward to certify that trees had been sold or 'assigned'. Any person found in possession of timber without this mark was liable to have some very awkward questions to answer. Equally true, Cobb knew, was that anyone found in possession of a replica was also likely to be in for a difficult time.

He asked Elizabeth what she knew about it and learnt how it came to be made. Her father, Thomas Johnson had been helping an underkeeper of Fritham Bailiwick, John Osland, in watching hawks in the early part of 1611. He had returned to his house one day carrying a chip cut from a tree which bore the woodward's mark. Johnson visited his brother Richard, in Southampton, mentioning to him that he had some lock stocks for the smith. He also couldn't resist telling him that he was going to get a marking axe made. He took the chip to a young locksmith, Richard Figgins in Southampton, and asked him to make a replica marking axe. Figgins, then aged twenty-three, had set up at New Corner opposite the *Dolphin*, where French Street joined English Street (now the High Street), a couple of years earlier. Perhaps lacking experience of the world and glad of the work he had not been too suspicious, and merely asked who it was for. Johnson told him that it was for his (unnamed) master who had lost the original.

This satisfied the craftsman and during the course of the following week he produced the replica for which he charged Johnson 2s 6d (12½p). It was returned, however, by Johnson as it didn't cut evenly and he produced a paper pattern for Figgins use. Elizabeth Johnson collected the improved version a week later which worked well enough to satisfy her father.

Elizabeth claimed that her father only used it to mark a couple of trees in Bratley Wood which he sold to an unnamed man from Ringwood. In fact, the master that he worked for was a timber merchant by the name of Thomas White. When John Norden had surveyed the forest for the king around 1608/9, the work was paid for, as was the custom, by the felling of timber. Much of this timber was bought by White. On his death bed Thomas Johnson had asked his daughter to bury the axe so that it might never be used again. Her uncle, Richard Johnson, had requested that she give it to him. She did neither and it remained hidden in the thatch until Nicholas Cobb found it. Nicholas, at some risk, took it, with other old iron, to his cottage where it remained untouched for over a year.

On his way through Wootton Coppice on the morning of Friday 6 May 1614, unable to keep the secret to himself any longer, he told his companion, Phillip Stryde, the whole story. Stryde, twenty-five years older than Cobb at fifty-five, and also a charcoal burner from Minstead, had the wisdom to advise him to come clean with the business and tell the authorities. He wanted him to take it to the Woodward of the Forest. Later that day they met the Woodward's servant, Francis Bennett, to whom they repeated the tale. He wanted the axe delivered straight away to his master. Cobb was unable to do that due to other business but did deliver it into the hands of the Woodward at his house in Holbury on the following Sunday.

This started a train of events that led to a full scale enquiry about the Norden sale of timber. Apart from Johnson and the timber dealer White, it was clear from witnesses' statements that John Osland the underkeeper was heavily involved. It may well have been on his suggestion that the axe was forged in the first place, he certainly made free use of the timber and knew how to falsify a mark. He boasted about the method he used: he chipped out an area of the tree near the root, then urinated on some green moss before applying it to the tree where the mark should be. In ten days it looked as if it had been there a year. Although perhaps not as vigilant as he might have been, no blame was attached to the Woodward.

And the name of the Woodward? – William Christmas.

Acknowledgements to Richard Reeves for research material.

Hollying

Forest Gypsies and Woodmen have cut holly for the Christmas market for generations. Here, the artist and archaeologist, Heywood Sumner, describes the process in his *Guide to the New Forest* first published in 1924.

Railway travellers during the month of December may see truck-loads of crimson-berried holly-tops standing in the sidings of the Forest stations, and may wonder how this wintry harvest of the woods is managed. 'Hollying' begins at the end of November. The holly trees are chosen and their tops cut by the woodman in each Walk. Then the small holder who has undertaken to buy the holly in this or that Walk, cuts up the tops into 'Forest faggots', for which he pays the Crown at so much per hundred, and carts them to the nearest place of despatch. This continues day by day for a fortnight. Then all the holly faggots for the London market are sent by train to Nine Elms Yard, where they are sold to the retailers. In late years, the war, high wages, high railway freight charges, and artificial holly have 'spoilt the trade', so it is said. Lopping holly trees in their prime of beauty may provoke the Forest lover, but the crop is needed, the hollies are abundant, while pollarding probably prolongs their ultimate age and results in picturesque growth.

By the 1930s the trade was back on its feet as is shown by Janet E. Case, a columnist for the *Manchester Guardian* who lived in Minstead. Her diary entry for 23 December, 1933 is entitled 'Gone the Holly'.

Where are the holly berries? Gone, I hope, to make Christmas gay for people in town. There are none left here. Their disappearance was so sudden and so complete it left us gasping. Probably the birds had an extra share in that sharp spell of cold weather, but the regular cutting was certainly more drastic than ever. What a harvest! One day a brilliant spectacle of crowded scarlet berries, the next not a glimmer of red. Cartloads have gone from here. There is not a berried twig overlooked or one branch with a berry on it in the heaps of discarded green. Only a few loose berries on the ground to mark where a tree stood. The children have ransacked the bushes for a bit to hang over the pictures or stick in the plum-pudding.

The Christmas Holly Cart by Myles Birket Foster

Christmas Menu in the Workhouse, 1847

The 1834 Poor Law Act grouped parishes together into unions in order to spread the cost to individual villages of the care of their needy. Union workhouses were built to house the poor and destitute and also gave 'out-relief' to others who could prove their need. The New Forest Union Workhouse, now Ashurst Hospital, was built on 6 acres of waste forest land in 1837 and united the parishes of Eling, Lyndhurst, Minstead, Bramshaw, Beaulieu, Fawley, Exbury and Dibden.

The workhouse was a last resort for those already used to extreme privation. Eager for the system not to appear an 'easy option', the government imposed strict regulations. Clothing was plain and food basic; married couples were separated and all slept in dormitories in the most primitive conditions. With high walls and exercise areas, the whole atmosphere must have been extremely prison-like. Inmates could, of course, discharge themselves but were then not eligible to return. Some were forced into the workhouse because of illness or infirmity, others were single mothers, homeless or unemployed.

In 1847 the New Forest Union Workhouse housed over two hundred people. The Master was George Horatio Miall and the Matron was his wife Jane. Miall's salary was £40 per annum. There was a schoolmaster, Thomas Whitehorn and a schoolmistress, Jane Davis who between them attempted to teach and control over one hundred children of varying ages; a seemingly impossible task.

Records show the average cost of providing for each inmate was 2s 11d per week. A normal weekly allowance of food per person was 9ozs cheese, 14ozs meat, 3lbs potatoes, 6lbs flour and 1 pint of beer or porter. During Christmas week the New Forest Union workhouse menu was enlivened with 30lbs of suet, 12lbs of raisins, 20lbs of currants and 1lb of spice and the meat consumption doubled. A morning service would have been read by the chaplain, the Reverend Mark Cooper from Bramshaw and some effort was probably made to decorate the bare walls.

If they were very lucky, local benefactors would provide small treats such as tea, sugar, nuts, tobacco and cake and sometimes small gifts for the children.

The Lymington Union comprised the parishes of Boldre, Brockenhurst, Hordle, Lymington, Milford, Milton, Rhinefield and Sway. An extract from *The New Forest Magazine*, January 1893, gives an account of a 'Christmas Treat' (Christmas came a little late that year) given to the inmates of Lymington workhouse which was situated in New Lane.

Treat to the Workhouse Inmates

On Monday evening, 16 Jan, the inmates of the Workhouse spent a very happy time together, a treat being provided for them by the Mayoress (Mrs Hill). Tea was first served in the chapel, which presented a gay spectacle, the Christmas decorations not having been removed. There was a plentiful supply of cakes, buns etc; and the pleasure of the poor people was greatly enhanced by the presence of the Mayoress and the Misses Hill, who were accompanied by a numerous party of friends, all of whom assisted the Master and Matron (Mr and Mrs Tuck) in looking after the wants of the guests of the evening. The meal proved a very merry time, and at its conclusion preparations were at once made for an evening's entertainment of music and recitations... There was also a distribution of sweets, oranges, crackers, tobacco etc, etc; the Mayoress personally handing the presents to the old people, and accompanying them with a kindly word to each recipient. Before the gathering was brought to a termination, the Vicar and Rural Dean (Rev. B. Maturin MA) said a few words, and called upon the guests to shew their appreciation of the kindly thoughtfulness of the Mayoress in entertaining them so pleasantly and merrily by three hearty cheers – and a lusty response was immediately made.

As the above shows, the end of the nineteenth century saw an emergence of a more humanitarian – albeit rather patronising – approach to the treatment of the poor. The following extract, however, taken from *The New Forest Magazine*, December 1894, gives evidence of a desire for real change.

For District Councillors, men are badly wanted who mean to leave no stone unturned until the present workhouse system is a thing of the past. The old married couples must live together as a matter of course, and only be separated at their own wish. The hateful custom of condemning the inmates to wear a uniform like criminals should be abolished with all reasonable speed; a more Christian system of leave out requires instant introduction; the too common plan of retaining children in the house should be universally abolished, and many other improvements are urgently required that we may be able to regain our self-respect as a Christian nation... No honest man begrudges a few pence in the pound to help our aged poor to end their days in common comfort and like human beings, and the system which condemns children to live in the workhouse re-acts upon itself with an inexorable vengeance; it fills to the full the annals of our crime, and the ranks of our pauper population. May God send us men throughout our land with brains to think, hearts to feel, and wills and power to dare and do.

The workhouses remained until the Poor Law Act was repealed in 1929.

Ashurst Hospital, formerly the New Forest Union Workhouse

Hard Winters

The New Forest has often been described as infertile heathland interspersed with heavily forested lowland and bog. Against this background the hardy Commoner has struggled for centuries to scratch his living from the soil. When nature is kind, the life is not a bad one. With the coming of winter, however, the true spirit of the Forester is tested. For centuries they have augmented their diet with venison. Punishment for taking the king's deer was harsh, but the need to provide for their families often outweighed the fear of being caught, literally, 'red-handed'. Ancient documents of the Swainmote court give evidence of countless actions brought against Foresters for poaching and, not surprisingly, the winter months saw many such offences. This example is taken from David Stagg's *Calendar of New Forest Documents* (15th-17th centuries), published in 1983.

> **40.** *Also that in the months of November, December and January 1485-6 the same William Edmond had entered the forest at various times and places, namely at Acres Down and Ocknell in the said bailiwick, and with greyhounds he had killed four young hinds, and had carried away the flesh without warrant or permission.*

Severe winters are by no means uncommon in the Forest despite our 'southerly' location. The 'Great Frost' of 1683-4, famous as the year when the Thames froze and streets of shopping booths were set up on the ice, also affected the south coast. It is described in the parish registers of Holy Rood, Southampton.

> *1683-4. This yeare was a great Frost, which began before Christmasse, soe that ye 3rd and 4th dayes of this month of February ye River of Southampton was frossen all over and covered with ice from Calshott Castle to Redbridge, and Tho: Martaine mariner of a vessell went upon ye ice from Berry near Marchwood to Millbrook-point. And ye river at Itchen Ferry was so frossen over that severall persons went from Beauvois-hill to Bitterne Farme forwards and backwards.*

Another example of a severe winter which took its toll on wildlife is to be found in John Wise's classic book *The New Forest, its History and Scenery*. The book was first published in 1863 and this account is of a hard winter that occurred seventy-five years earlier.

One tradition ought to be told concerning the terrible winter of 1787, still known in the Forest as the hard year'. My informant, an old man, derived his knowledge from his father, who lived in the Forest in a small lonely farm-house. The storm began in the night; and when his father rose in the morning he could not, on account of the snow-drift, open the door. Luckily, a back room had been converted into a fuel-house, and his wife had laid in a stock of provisions. The storm still increased. The straggling hedges were soon covered; and by-and-by the woods themselves disappeared. After a week's snow, a heavy frost followed. The snow hardened. People went out shooting, and wherever a breathing-hole in the snow appeared, fired, and nearly always killed a hare. The snow continued on the ground for seven weeks; and when it melted, the stiffened bodies of horses and deer covered the plains. In that winter three hundred deer were starved to death in Boldrewood Walk alone.

In 1881 Charles W. Wood came to the New Forest and he wrote an article called 'In the New Forest' which appeared in *Argosy* magazine in February of that year.

One night, darkness fell upon a green world... The next morning... everyone was amazed to find the world white. Through the night the silent and unseasonable visitor had fallen thick and fast, and was falling still.

It seemed no time for prolonging one's sojourn in the New Forest. I felt inclined to pack up and depart. The old postman - the most popular of all public characters – when he arrived with the letters, said the snow was so thick upon the trees that branches were breaking in all directions with the report of small guns. But presently the snow ceased, the leaden sky rolled away, the sun came out with all the brightness it wears on such occasions.

Improving the opportunity, I started for a long ride in company with my good host, without whose guidance I should quickly have gone astray in the mazes and thickets we proposed to explore. I was again mounted upon the little Pride of the Forest, and as he tossed his head, and snapped at the stirrups and reared in the exuberance of his youthful spirits, it was evident that he meant to have his own share of fun and enjoyment out of the afternoon.

We were bound for Mark Ash, almost the finest part of the New Forest: though where all is so beautiful comparison seems invidious. It would be difficult to describe the wild grandeur of the wood after we entered within the bounds of Boldrewood and Mark Ash… High above our heads, meeting like the Gothic arches of a Cathedral, wide branches spread and blended together. Often we stood enclosed as by walls, in these natural temples, the trees standing out from each other in long and lovely aisles for a great distance, the sky but not the daylight completely shut out. Every branch was lined with snow; everything was white and dazzling; the barer branches ran in white veins, and clung and clasped each other like things of life. A white fretwork was above and around us.

Branches, some of them as large as small trees, lay prone upon the earth, borne down by the weight of the snow, and obstructing our path. Even as we stood, wondering silently at all this strange beauty, branches cracked and fell to the earth – as the old postman had said – with the report of small guns.

A series of cold winters between 1938 and 1942, and again in 1947, proved problematic to birds and other wildlife as well as to humans; while the prolonged spell of freezing weather between December 1962 and March 1963 saw the death of three hundred deer and ponies and all but exterminated the Dartford Warbler and wren populations.

A New Forest Cottage near Lyndhurst by Barry Peckham

It was a lonely winter's eve;
The moon's pale beaming light
Shone brightly forth, so soft, so clear,
So calmly through the atmosphere,
That all on earth, both far and near,
Look'd pure and silv'ry bright!

from *The Wounded Stag*,
P Klitz, *New Forest Sketches*, 1850

Christmas Gypsy Craft

New Forest gypsies would make wax flowers at Christmas time 'planting' them in little pots with wax leaves which looked extraordinarily lifelike. They also made flowers from paper and rushes and a few, like Lavinia Cooper, would whittle beautiful flowers out of wood and dye them all colours. Painted crab-apples and silver-dipped 'butcher's broom' also made pretty decorations. New Forest gypsies were not, traditionally, van dwellers. They lived in bender tents or tans which consisted of tarpaulin stretched over bent hazel rods. This outdoor life made them extremely hardy, and able to withstand the rigours of winter, as H. E. J. Gibbins noted in 1909.

> *I have seen but few of them ill, and have never met one in a tent suffering from rheumatism. Colds they have at times, but not half so badly as house-dwellers; and bronchitis – or, as they persist in calling it, 'the Brown Kitis' – is perhaps unknown, except amongst their baby children, and in these so-called cases I think it is more often only a cold, so magnified for the purpose of invoking charity.*

Gypsies at Thorneyhill lived 'in the hollies' and the hollies, as well as providing shelter, furnished a means of livelihood at Christmas. The flower-sellers made wreaths and took bunches of mistletoe and red-berried holly from door to door or sold them on their rounds in the nearby towns.

The roads are very dirty, my shoes are very thin,
I have a little pocket to put my money in.
Your pocket full of money, your cellar full of beer,
I wish you a Merry Christmas and a Happy New Year.

Traditional gypsy song

New Forest Calendar December

Sylvia Oldroyd is a published and prize-winning poet who lives on the Waterside. She paints evocative pictures with her words as can be seen in the following poem which comes from her *New Forest Calendar* series.

DECEMBER
by Sylvia Oldroyd

Razored by frost,
The week's enduring overcast
is shorn for this yearly ritual,
as we thread our way along
Quobb Gutter, counting off
each known way-mark,
gate-post, tree, lane-winding;
leaned on, sheltered under, followed
through a lifetime of seasons.

Oak mittens shurr underfoot,
furred with rime in the open places.
Field-grass is starched to attention,
massed spears challenge
the hooves of cattle encircling
piled hay; breath rises
in a silent psalm of praise.

Figures from a Victorian print,
in a resinous aura we carry
the tree between us; rest
by a bramble-clump,
head-high pyramid streamered
in red-stemmed briars, hung
with blown-glass beads.
Tinsel sparks glance
off icicled thorns.

At home, we raise
our evergreen deity
in the window-corner,
arms outstretched
to welcome in the solstice;
to celebrate the coming
of the light.

Ho, Ho, Ho!
the Wild Wind Blows

The following Christmas song appeared in the December 1894 edition of the *New Forest Parish Magazine*. Most of the New Forest Parishes sent in reports of the village news – Baptisms, Marriages etc; – and details of outings, meetings and forthcoming events. It was not uncommon in Victorian times to perform church ceremonies at Christmas. At St Mary's, Copythorne, for example Lily Gould of Newbridge and Elsie Andrews of Ower were baptised on Christmas Day as was Sarah Moncton at Dibden Church; Richard Martin, aged ninety, of Ashlett Creek 'one of the oldest and most respected inhabitants' of Fawley Parish was buried on Boxing Day.

The magazine, which had one hundred subscribers in 1893, (approximately three years after it first appeared) was still being published in the 1940s. In the early editions communications are directed to the General Editor, *New Forest Magazine*, Bank, Lyndhurst. This may well have been the novelist Mary Braddon, who lived with her publisher husband John Maxwell, in the house they had built in the early 1880s called *Annesley*, at Bank. Mary edited several other magazines during her literary career and she wrote at least two novels with a Forest background. *Vixen*, published in 1879, is the nickname of the young and spirited Violet Tempest who rides to hounds at the age of eleven and lives 'in an old manor house in the heart of the New Forest' and *Mount Royal*, the old name for Northerwood House near Lyndhurst, appeared in 1882.

'Ho, Ho, Ho! the Wild Winds Blow.'

CHRISTMAS SONG.

' Christmas comes! He comes, he comes,
Hollies in the window greet him.
Gifts precede him, bells proclaim him,
Every mouth delights to name him.'—LEIGH HUNT.

ARTHUR HENRY BROWN.

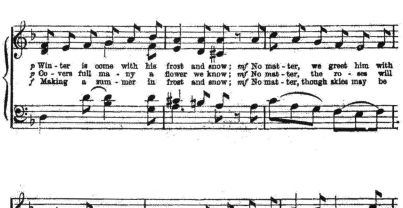

p Win - ter is come with his frost and snow; mf No mat - ter, we greet him with
p Co - vers full ma - ny a flower we know; mf No mat - ter, the ro - ses will
f Making a sum - mer in frost and snow; mf No mat - ter, though skies may be

song and cheer, f For mer - ry old Christmas a - gain is here. mp No
bloom a - gain, f To glow in the sun - shine and nod in the rain. mp No
dark a - bove, f There's sunshine of sum - mer in homes of love. mp No

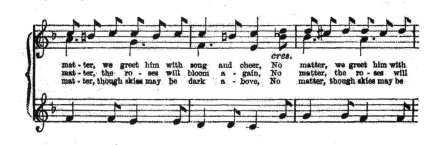

cres.

mat - ter, we greet him with song and cheer, No matter, we greet him with
mat - ter, the ro - ses will bloom a - gain, No matter, the ro - ses will
mat - ter, though skies may be dark a - bove, No matter, though skies may be

rall. . . . . ⌒   CHORUS, *tempo.*

song and cheer, For mer - ry old Christmas a - gain is here.
bloom a - gain, To glow in the sunshine and nod in the rain. f Ho, Ho, Ho! we'll
dark a - bove, There's sunshine of sum - mer in homes of love.

A Verderer's Christmas

BY PETER ROBERTS

The Verderers meet eleven times a year, on the third Monday of the month, and all except one of these meetings involves an open court. The 'Christmas Court' in December has a shortened programme of business to be attended to, always timed to finish by noon, to enable them to receive and entertain past Verderers and associates in an informal manner. It is an ideal opportunity to bend the ear of others without commitment and perhaps helps understanding of the other person's viewpoint without going through what might otherwise be a formal process. Whilst not degenerating into the wildest extremes of office parties, it is a relaxed occasion.

It is also the day on which the Verderers receive their annual 'payment'. Verderers have always been unpaid but there was a time-honoured tradition of right to any buck that happened

Queen's House, Verderer's Hall and Church, Lyndhurst

to cross his or her path on the way to Court. This has changed in modern times. None now carry bows and arrows to Lyndhurst, though they may think suitable targets still exist there. As compensation, a haunch of venison is now supplied to each Verderer at Christmas.

One Verderer, in the first year of his office, received his haunch early in the month and, not realising that it had already been hung for a while, hung it in the stairwell until Christmas Day. It provided a point of interest for all visitors; in particular one young vegetarian who bumped into it in the half dark one evening. She won't forget the occasion in a hurry.

It was thought that the venison would provide an interesting variation on turkey for Christmas Day lunch. Now it may have been hung more than necessary and it may have been cooked a little too long; certainly those friends and family whose teeth had seen seventy such festive seasons, struggled somewhat before abandoning the unequal fight in order to enjoy the vegetables and the Christmas pudding.

A Traditional
New Forest Recipe

BY IRENE SOPER

Roast Shoulder of Venison

2.5kg/5½ lb shoulder of venison

olive oil

1 clove garlic

sprig of rosemary

flour and butter for basting

Heat the oven to 200°C, 190°C for a fan oven or Gas Mark 6. Wipe the joint, brush with olive oil and wrap in foil and place in a roasting pan. Cook for one and a half hours, then remove the joint, open out the foil, flour the top of the meat, baste with butter and return to the oven to brown and froth for a further thirty minutes.

Serve with Alboni sauce, roast potatoes, French beans and leeks.

Alboni Sauce

100g/4oz butter

13g/½oz plain flour

1tbsp chopped parsley

2tbsp vinegar

salt and pepper to taste

1 large tbsp redcurrant jelly

Warm the butter in a saucepan until it melts, include the flour and brown. Then add the chopped parsley, vinegar and salt and pepper. Simmer for one minute and add the redcurrant jelly. Serve immediately. This makes a rich thick sauce, add a little red wine for a thinner consistency.

A Wanderer in
the New Forest

Juliette de Baïracli Levy, traveller, writer, botanist and herbalist was educated at Manchester and Liverpool universities. She came to the New Forest in the 1950s to live 'the natural life' in a primitive cottage thatched with straw and heather, at Abbots Well, near Godshill. Her friends were foresters, shepherds and, of course, the gypsies with whom she claims kinship. The following extract from her book *Wanderers in the New Forest*, published by Faber and Faber in 1958, gives the reader a sense of her intense understanding of, and her involvement with, the natural world.

Christmas in the New Forest always seemed to be distinguished by exceptional sunsets. That sky of a peculiar violet shade which I have not seen beyond the New Forest; and the bars of pink light striking across it, and Venus the evening star rising immense over the trees; all to be seen from the cottage windows as the first carols were sung.

Snow and frost over the forest which usually came after the Christmas weather changes, meant much extra toil for me as keeper of our primitive cottage with thatched roof and mud paths and snow blowing in on us through the door that I could never tolerate having closed until the cold of night came. I was compensated for the increased work by the likewise increased beauty that came with such weather. Snow piled in fair shapes on surrounding tree boughs and furze. The feet tracks of birds and forest animals made delicate lace patterns across newly-come snow, and the wind made ripple markings. Frost turned our window panes into pictures of massed silver ferns, and laid tinsel over everything. The wild birds came inside our cottage in increasing numbers and the ponies were at our gate seeking hay from my orchard's high grass and nettles which had once bedded our wind-fall apples, but which I had since scythed.

It is around every Christmas Eve and Day that Nature seems exceptionally active. The ancients were aware of this and those days seemed to have been celebrated by many non-Christian races before becoming a Christian religious festival. It is known that it were the Druids who originated the use of their magic herb, mistletoe, at Christmas time.

I have long sensed a deep stirring from the earth at that time, while the light in the sky grows on from then, and the tree boughs are made restive. Even the bees in their hives seem to awaken for those few days, and on Christmas Day I have often seen several bees leave a hive and flight around despite the cold usually prevailing.

Hard freezing brought the skaters to the flooded gravel-pit stretches near our cottage; and there was skating also on Windsmore pond when frost was severe enough to freeze over the depth that it usually possessed in mid-winter and early spring. Several families had portable gramophones with them to send music over the ice as they skated, though for me the running music of the quick skate-blades was pleasure enough. Pleasure also in the whirling patterns that the blades cut upon the ice surface.

Winter Skating by George Morland

A Forest Winter

A rtist, writer and teacher Allen W. Seaby, 1867 - 1953, was based in Reading but spent most of his holidays with his family in the New Forest. In 1923 he published *Skewbald, the New Forest Pony* and several other books with a Forest setting followed; *The White Buck* (1939), *Omrig and Nerla* (1934) and *Purkess the Charcoal Burner* (1946). He became Head of Reading College of Art and with colleagues Frank Morley Fletcher and John Dickson Batten pioneered the production of colour woodcut prints in England, using traditional Japanese methods. Seaby made nearly two hundred multi-colour woodcut prints, from small Christmas cards to bird studies and large landscapes.

In his book *British Ponies – Running Wild and Ridden* published by A. & C. Black in 1936, he describes, with the unmistakable eye of an artist, a winter moonlight stroll in the rides of Balmer Lawn at Brockenhurst; and in *Skewbald, the New Forest Pony* he describes how Skewbald's mother teaches her son the tricks that are needed to survive the rigours of a Forest winter.

Ponies grow a thick winter coat to protect them from the blast and foals quickly learn to nibble the young shoots of gorse before they become too prickly. Foresters cut holly for the ponies and they often congregate at the sites within minutes of the cutting, trampling on the holly to soften it before they eat. Foals lie in bracken for shelter and, when it rains, keep their backs to the wind to lessen the surface area exposed to the elements.

Another traveller and writer who loved the New Forest was Charles John Cornish, who was born in Sidmouth, Devon in 1858. Known professionally as C. J. Cornish, he became assistant classical master at St Paul's School, London in 1884. It was this appointment, giving the freedom of weekend and long seasonal breaks, that allowed Cornish to indulge his love of travelling in the countryside. He began to write natural history and country life articles and the first were published in *St James's Gazette* in 1886. By 1890 he was contributing a regular weekly article to the *Spectator* and later assisted in the foundation of the illustrated weekly *Country Life*.

Cornish married, in 1893, Edith Thornycroft whose father was a designer and builder of torpedo boats based at Chiswick and Bembridge on the Isle of Wight. It was this association that brought him to our southern shore and the publishing, in 1894, of his first book *The New Forest*. The following year he brought out *The Isle of Wight* and these are now often found bound in one volume.

In this extract from *The New Forest* Cornish gives his interpretation of how the hardy New Forest pony breed manages to survive the winter.

The history of these New Forest ponies is by no means ascertained. They are not an indigenous animal like the red deer, but the uniformity in size and appearance suggests a common stock and ancestry. The first is, however, probably due to the almost feral state in which these ponies live in the wild district, from which their food-supply is entirely obtained. No pony above a certain size is likely to survive in the forest, for the simple reason that it cannot find food to maintain it. In winter, by browsing all day and the greater part of the night, hardy little "foresters" of from twelve to thirteen hands high can just make both ends meet, though they are extremely thin and ragged.

But anything much above that size would need artificial support, and its progeny would deteriorate. On the other hand, their size does not tend to fall much below the standard at which Nature sets the limit, which, in the case of the New Forest pony, seems to be from twelve to thirteen and a half hands. The natural appetite and needs of these hardy creatures prompt them to do the best for themselves from day to day with a constancy hardly to be understood by human beings whose minds are not concentrated by necessity on the absorbing effort to satisfy the hourly cravings of hunger. Nature levels up as it levels down, and this is probably the clue to the uniformity in size of all wild animals, as well as of these half-wild ponies.

It must not be supposed, from the rough and poor condition of these creatures when seen in April, after exposure to the long hard winter, that their life is uniformly one of privation and hardship. The health and freedom which they enjoy together make them on the whole a very happy and contented race.

The Marlpit Oak Gibbet

Another chilling winter's tale from Desmond A. LePard, a master storyteller, who lives in Sway.

For many years, according to an old New Forest Legend, there stood at the crossroads, known as Marlpit Oak, on the high plain between Sway and Brockenhurst, a great double-armed gibbet. Visible for miles around, and frequently bearing a grisly load, it must have been a fearful sight, brooding over the remote and lonely countryside. It was, therefore, a matter of widespread satisfaction when, in the early part of the nineteenth century, the gibbet was at last demolished. However, superstition was very powerful in those far-off days and strange stories soon began to circulate among the Forest people.

When I was young and not long from school
Like all braggart youth I was brazen and brave,
And I laughed him to scorn and called him a fool
Who spoke of the dead that returned from the grave.

'When they are dead, they are dead – so much mouldering clay'
'And he who says not is drunk or insane!'
And the wager seemed nought in the bright light of day
To spend that night, alone, by the knoll on the plain.

By the time evening came and the winter sun set
In a great blood-red glow over Wilverley Hill,
Every soul in the village had heard of the bet,
And my arrogant heart had felt the first chill.

For I knew the story, like all of us there,
Of the Marlpit Oak Gibbet which, many years gone,

Had stood, high and grim, in the very place where
I'd boasted I'd spend the whole night alone.

A hillock of bare earth is all that remains
Standing just a few yards from the well-trodden way
Which, crossing the miles of gorse-covered plain,
Brings the traveller at last to the village of Sway.

Even in Spring, when the moorland glows gold,
And the warm-scented furze calls the foraging bees,
The ground at this place stays mortally cold
And no skylark nests here, no pony takes ease.

No sun-loving lizard, no close-crouching hare,
No adder, loose-coiled, seeks this chilly mound.
No beast of the Forest, no bird of the air,
No grass, gorse or heather, is here to be found.

And a tale was told by the old men of Sway
Of a travelling merchant who would not take heed,
Who had to reach Lyndhurst by early next day
And who swore his two pistols were all that he'd need.

They said he was found with his hair turned quite white,
Eyes fixed and staring, and mouth open wide,
Silently screaming at some ghastly sight,
And no mark on his body to show how he died.

Just tales? Superstitions of foolish old men?
But my heart filled with terror that pride would not show,
And I drank deep and waited the dread moment when
Someone would say it was time now to go.

Too soon came the moment, and into the night
Drunken and singing we lurched through the snow,
All close round the lantern, whose pale yellow light

In the menacing darkness cast scarcely a glow.

And I sung the loudest of all of us there,
And shouted with laughter at each feeble jest,
And I threw out the challenge that I didn't care
If the Devil himself came - He'd soon give me best!

And then we were there, and the merriment died
As, suddenly sober, we stood in the snow,
But still I obeyed my obstinate pride
And in confident tones urged the others to go.

The sound of their voices died quickly away,
The gleam of the lantern was soon lost to sight,
As they hurried thankfully back home to Sway,
To bolt cottage doors and to shut out the night.

The air, when the snow stopped, was bitterly cold,
The darkness intense, the stillness profound,
And the whole world was silent as, no longer bold,
I fearfully stood by the old Gibbet mound.

Trembling, I looked to the left and the right,
While the terrible cold froze me through to the bone,
Then I suddenly knew, though no soul was in sight,
That, beyond any doubt, I was not alone!

How can I describe that unreasoning fear,
That primitive terror no thought can prevent,
Of knowing that someone, or something, was near,
And directing at me its evil intent.

Filled with blind panic, I turned and I fled,
Stumbling and sobbing and cursing the night,
Until, just as my strength was beginning to ebb,
Far ahead I discerned a faint glimmer of light.

Faltering now, and filled with despair,
Like a desperate fox hunted over the moor,
Heart beating wildly, and gasping for air,
I staggered at last to the furze-cutter's door.

Exhausted, defeated, I sank to my knees,
A pitiful, tremulous, cowering wreck.
And then, with infinite horror, I felt
Long bony fingers encircling my neck.

I remember no more – I fainted away
With that fearful pressure unbearably tight,
And they say that I lay there, half-dead, half-alive,
Till the furze-cutter came in the grey morning light.

I'm told that for weeks I was kept to my bed,
Mumbling and muttering and never quite sane,
Then at last came the Spring, and with it my strength,
And I became part of the village again.

But the fear has remained, throughout my long life,
And I sometimes awake in the depths of the night
And though it be Summer my blood turns to ice,
And I cry out in terror as reason takes flight.

I was only a boy but my memory stays clear
Of that dreadful night, now so far and remote.
But you don't believe me? Then what is this scar,
This ring of dead flesh like a noose round my throat?

And who among you, on this black Winter night,
When the fog is so thick and the village snowbound,
Will go out from his house, leave the fire and the light,
And keep vigil, alone, by the old gibbet mound?

Boxing Day
Point-to-Point

Many circular point-to-point races, with jumps, are run in rural areas all over Britain. The New Forest Boxing Day point-to-point is unique in that it still runs on the original lines – no jumps, and starting from one point in the Forest to another. The starting point is kept secret until Christmas Day, when riders and owners are told where to assemble. The approximate finishing point is published a week or so beforehand in the local press. Occasionally it is cancelled when weather is extreme and the lives of the ponies and riders would be at risk. The race tests both the pony's stamina and the rider's knowledge of Forest terrain as they must choose the shortest and safest route between the two points. Here, Stuart 'Geordie' Cooke describes a Boxing Day point-to-point in his children's book *A Forest Friendship*, published in 1991.

Stuart Cooke is a New Forest Commoner and retired Agister. In his book, Jane Taylor, a ten year-old asthmatic, moves from London to the New Forest. Bewildered, at first, by the enormous change in her life, she befriends a mare she calls 'Star' and later Star's foal, Blackie. When Star is killed in a road accident, Jane is distraught until they find a foster-mother for Blackie. Blackie thrives and so does Jane, her asthma becoming only a memory. Four years later Jane rides Blackie in the Boxing Day point-to-point.

The forecast for Boxing Day had been good – slight frost in the early morning, with the sun breaking through by mid-morning. Today she was to ride Blackie in the point-to-point races, an event organised by the New Forest Pony Breeding and Cattle Society, always held, weather permitting, on Boxing Day morning. The race is unique in the fact that no-one, including owners and riders, is told of the starting point until twenty-four hours before the race, although they are told of the vicinity of the finish.

The Course Setter had telephoned Jane on Christmas Morning to tell her the start would be near Beaulieu Road railway station. Jane already knew the finish would be at Poundhead, Lyndhurst, and that the riders would not be allowed to follow the main road, but had to keep to the heath and woodlands of the forest.

Jane was beginning to feel nervous as she thought about the race and the accidents that often occurred. When they arrived, the adult competitors were being weighed and their animals measured ready to take part in their particular race. The races for children under seventeen years of age were exempt from that rule.

Jane gets advice from her friend, the Agister, Bill Balfour:

'When the race starts, don't go too fast. There are ten in your race and, if possible, try to keep about fourth or fifth. Then when you are through Matley Wood, let Blackie have his head. Be careful when you are galloping over the bridge, you know, the one you can see from the Pony Sale yard.'

The white flag is dropped and the race begins. Another horse and rider take a fall on the first bridge and then Jane's friend Emily falls victim to the notorious channels on Big Matley. Emily is unhurt and urges Jane on. Blackie carries her swiftly on and soon she is locked in a battle with her rival, James Osborne on his pony, Tornado, in Matley Bog:

Jane was about to enter Queen's Passage, about four metres wide with bogs on either side, when, out of the corner of her eye she caught another glimpse of James's pony galloping very fast towards her. Blackie and Tornado reached the entrance to the Passageway together. Tornado appeared to stumble, and he caught Blackie on his off-side shoulder causing him to lose balance and fall on his knees by the edge of the bog. Blackie fought to regain his hold – both forelegs had slipped into the bog. He was frightened and began to panic, but Jane, determined to keep calm, said:

'It's all right Blackie, good boy, good boy.'

At the sound of her voice, Blackie pivoted on his hind legs that luckily were still on firmer ground, pulling his forelegs free from the bog.

Jane and Blackie race on through Matley Wood and over the heath catching up with James and Tornado – and, of course, passing them – within sight of the finishing line.

Gibbins Redbreast

enry E. J. Gibbins was a champion of New Forest gypsies. He founded The New Forest Good Samaritan Charity to help gypsy families and other poor parishioners. In 1909 he published a book of his experiences with the gypsies called *Gipsies of the New Forest and Other Tales*. The dedication comes, unusually, at the end of the book:

Dedicated,
with my most earnest wish for their betterment,
to the outcasts of Civilisation –

'The Gipsies.'
'To whom Sun and Wind mean much;
But Freedom means much more.'

The book also contains tales of smuggling and poaching, anecdotes and poetry, written mostly by Gibbins himself. The poem below appears on page 105 and is very twee, but is disarmingly countered by the quote which follows it.

GIPSIES
OF THE
NEW FOREST
AND
OTHER TALES

BY

H. E. J. G.

ILLUSTRATED.
PRICE 2/6 NET.

PUBLISHED BY
W. MATE & SONS, LTD.,
BOURNEMOUTH, LYMINGTON, &c.

COCK ROBIN

Who does not love Cock Robin?
The children's darling pet;
Who hops upon our window sill,
A closer peep to get.

At early morn he pays his call,
The children's loving smile to greet:
At noon he welcomes one and all,
And pipes at eve 'Au revoir, sweet.'

Of all the feathered tribes we know,
He gains the most esteem;
His ruddy breast is all aglow,
Of him the children dream.

Cock Robin and the tiny Wren
Are to the children dear:
And friendliest seem of all the birds,
When Christmas time draws near.

When white the garden is with snow,
And frost binds hard the ground:
These little pets their instinct show,
And nearer hop around.

With trustful look and earnest glance,
They search the crumbs to find;
Whilst children in the nursery dance,
And gaze with looks so kind.

The day is drawing to its close,
Cock Robin bobs his head:
And in bird language means to say,
By-bye, I'm off to bed.

H.E.J.G.

Buffon, the great French naturalist, in his writings says of Robin Redbreast, 'This amiable little warbler is eaten with bread crumbs.' Alas! for the taste; had he said *fed* with bread crumbs it would have been better.

Wassailing

Wassailing fruit trees is an ancient custom connected with Christmas and New Year. The word wassail is from the Saxon 'Was Hal' and means 'Good Luck' or 'Be in Good Health'. In order to rid the trees of evil spirits which may affect the following year's crop, country folk would assemble in the orchard after dark with pails of cider or ale. Here, they would form rings round the trees and sing traditional songs, like those below, and then drink a toast to the trees.

The following extract, written by J. H. King, appeared in Vol 1 of the *Hampshire Antiquary and Naturalist* published in 1891, and describes the New Forest version of the wassail.

A CHRISTMAS EVE CUSTOM

In the New Forest it is customary on Christmas Eve for the inhabitants to assemble under the trees and drink ale together, singing the following rhyme:-

> *Apples and pears with right good corn*
> *Come in plenty to everyone,*
> *Eat and drink good cake and hot ale*
> *Give earth to drink and she'll not fail.*

Chambers's Book of Days

This custom appears to resemble that of wassailing, a very old custom prevailing in Devonshire and elsewhere, and appears to be a relic of an old pagan custom and belief that fruit trees were rendered more fruitful by this invocation, as shown by the following old rhyme:-

> *Wassail the trees, that they may bear*
> *You many a plum and many a pear*
> *For more or less fruit they will bring*
> *As you do them wassailing.*

The words 'give earth to drink' in the New Forest rhyme show that it was customary to pour ale on the ground as a libation to the earth, while in the Devonshire 'wassailing' a cup of cider is thrown at the trees.

Traditional weather lore gives more substance to the view that it is important to have a fine Christmas Day to ensure a good crop. Late frosts kill apple blossom and ruin crops, and a sunny Christmas means a frost-free May and a good autumn.

Sun through the apple trees on Christmas day,
Means a fine crop is on the way.

Tragedy at Christmas, 1878

BY PETER ROBERTS

In the Churchyard at Colbury there is an unusual stone depicting a train marking the untimely death of Charles Shave.

Mr Shave was born in Ringwood in 1837, he married Dorcas, a girl from Preston Candover and lived in the Ringwood area until 1861. When he moved to the eastern side of the Forest at Hounsdown he took up the job, which he was to hold for seventeen years, of assistant gateman at the nearby Lyndhurst Road Station. (Now Ashurst, New Forest.)

The station wasn't quite by the gate, a point of some irritation to the directors of the Southampton and Dorchester Railway who would have preferred an adjacent site to avoid additional staffing costs. It was placed approximately a hundred yards to the south. The Commissioners of Woods, who managed the Forest on behalf of the Crown, had the final say on its position. A small shelter had been built for the gateman close to the house of the gatekeeper, John Gain, on the north or down side of the line. Apart from opening the gates to the public on the road between Eling and Lyndhurst, the gateman's task was to signal the trains passing through.

The evening of Monday 23 December 1878 brought a heavy frost, Mr Shave's shift which started at 8pm was going to be a long cold one. His colleague, Frank Browning, the parcels porter at the station, chatted to him for over an hour before they parted at 11.30. Although it was Christmas they were both on duty and conscientious workers so did not have a drink. That was to be the last time Charles Shave was seen alive.

At thirteen minutes past twelve, having left his box on the other side of the line, Charles Shave signalled the up-train as was the normal procedure to indicate all was well. He then put the lamp down, perhaps to tie his shoe, maybe to examine something or do his coat up, and then returned to his box leaving his lamp on the side of the track. He was slow coming out for the down-train half an hour later. Hearing the train coming and knowing it was his duty to signal it he hurried across the rails to retrieve his lamp. Unfortunately due to the frost the rails were slippery, he fell and was struck by the train and dragged 25 yards down the line. The driver of the train saw and heard nothing, perhaps just mentally noting that the gateman had dozed off and so failed to signal him.

His injuries were horrific causing death instantaneously. Mr Shave had arranged to call Charles Bessant, another porter, at a quarter-to-six and had even chalked a note to that effect on the wall of his box. Upon Shave's non appearance Bessant went to his box, found the door open, the message on the wall and the fire out before discovering the body between the rails. Boxing Day at the New Forest Union was a sombre affair, for Mr Harfield the Coroner held his inquest there during which the circumstances were carefully examined and a verdict of accidental death was returned.

Lyndhurst Road Station, now Ashurst (New Forest), where Charles Shave died.

In winter, the Forest, be-jewelled and enmossed
becomes a fairyland of frost
The air so still you can hear each sound
each footfall on the crisp, hard ground
Deer flee, as fast as they are able
unwilling to be venison on a Verderer's table
And if snow comes – wrapped up, fingers clenched
children toboggan on Bolton's Bench.

Fig Pudding and Ginger Wine

The two recipes below were found in a manuscript book during a recent house clearance in the east of the Forest. There are two dates in the book – December 1845 and 1892 – and the hand-written entries, some in beautiful copperplate, appear to be in different hands, perhaps passed down through the family. As well as recipes the book contains the ingredients for making polish, a cement to mend china and hints on how to clean marble mantelpieces.

Fig Pudding

Three quarters of a pound of grated bread, half a pound of the best figs, six ounces of suet, six ounces of moist sugar, a teacupful of milk, a little nutmeg.

The figs and suet must be chopped very fine. Mix the bread and suet first, then the figs, sugar and nutmeg, 1 egg well beaten and lastly the milk. Boil in a mould 4 hours. Eaten with sweet sauce.

Ginger Wine

To each gallon of water 3lbs of loaf sugar 1oz of White Ginger 3 lemons – boil them till the scum is all taken off well then pour the boiling liquor upon the rinds of the lemons. When it is nearly cold put the juice of the lemons and a teaspoonful of new yeast into the cask. Let it work two or three days, then add to it a little Brandy – bottle it in six weeks if you choose.

Christmas Ghosts at the Fox and Hounds

T he Fox and Hounds, situated prominently in Lyndhurst High Street, is an old coaching inn of historical note, possibly dating back further than the eighteenth century.

Lyndhurst High Street, with the Fox and Hounds *in the centre, by John G Short, c.1900.*
Photo courtesy of the New Forest Ninth Centenary Trust Library and Resource Centre

In the middle of the nineteenth century the landlord was John Ives and he was to gain an unenviable celebrity. The following extract is from an article by Rosemary A. Manning which appeared in *Nova Foresta Magazine*, Vol 2 No.1, in 1996.

Landlords, Fire and Ghosts

John Ives's notoriety came from the tragic accident which killed him in the New Year of 1867. The gruesome article in the Hampshire Advertiser *of Saturday 5 January, 1867 was headed:*

The Landlord of the Fox and Hounds Burnt to Death

It was an account of the inquest held on the premises before Mr B. Harfield, the then deputy Coroner on Thursday 3 January, 1867. The events unfolded as follows:

Ann Ives, the deceased's wife, told the Deputy Coroner that her husband was sixty. Apparently on New Year's Day (a Tuesday), she and the late John Ives had been together in the bar a little before 3 o'clock in the afternoon. She left him in the room and on returning ten minutes later, noticed an unusual light under the door. She opened the door only to find her husband 'sitting on the ground', his head somehow on the bars of the grate. He had his back to the fire and his clothes were alight. Mrs Ives shouted 'Fire!' and tried to lift her husband. She told the inquest that he did not speak. A guest, stonemason John Baker, came in with a bucket of water and threw it over the burning man. They were by now able to move him to another room, and still he did not speak. William Wallace, Dr Maskew's assistant did all he could to save the horribly burnt, dying man. John Baker stayed with Ives until he died at 'twenty minutes to four o'clock on Wednesday morning.' The witness said in evidence that the only thing uttered by the poor man was that his 'game leg had given out.' Apparently this had happened on other occasions without such dire results.

It was stated also at the inquest that John Baker thought that although Ives was 'conscious of all that was passing around him', he probably was not aware that he had been burnt. As far as he knew the deceased had had only one glass of spirits during the day. William Wallace, the doctor's assistant said that Ives had 'extensive burns on both the back and front of his body.' Dr Maskew gave evidence that death was undoubtedly due to the severe burns and the shock thereof. Dr Maskew thought that he 'might have fallen in a fit.' The verdict returned was that John Ives was 'accidentally burnt to death.'

Tom and Vicky Miles, who have hosted the Fox and Hounds since 1993, had never heard the story of John Ives, when I revealed it to them as we sat comfortably in the bar one day.

'Well that could explain it,' said Vicky, looking across at her husband as he simultaneously began to speak.

Tom told me that they had heard the Inn was haunted, but had not taken a lot of notice. 'Everything is alright 99% of the time' he added. It emerged that, always around Christmas and the New Year, there were unexplained phenomena.

In the kitchen there is an industrial gas oven with a knob on the front which is very hard to turn. A smell of gas coming from the kitchen revealed that the knob had been turned 180 degrees. This was strange because the chef had checked it and there is also a security check. The gas had been inexplicably turned on more than once after more security checks.

Tom said also the cellarman complained of occasionally finding the water tap running in the cellar after he was certain he had turned it off. Not just dripping – but running, so that it could be heard from upstairs. Vicky also mentioned flickering lights and all this happening only around the New Year.

'Was there really a ghost?' I asked Tom. He replied that all he could say was that an Australian psychic had been sleeping in the front bedroom, when he awoke to find a lady dressed in black looking down the High Street.

Ivy and Mistletoe

The following extracts are from Juliette de Baïracli Levy's chapter on 'Herbs of the New Forest' which appeared in *The New Forest: A Symposium* published by the Galley Press in 1960.

Ivy (Hedera helix) *is another famed herb suffering unjustly under the ill reputation of being 'evil' and poisonous. Ivy berries are an ancient fever cure; they are also an excellent tonic for poultry. The bees at least honour the ivy plant and swarm to its honey so rich in nerve-tonic properties. Sheep, goats, cattle and deer also flock to ivy to eat its foliage with relish. They know how much to take, for when overeaten it can prove harmful. It is not a safe food for ewes in lamb, who are apt to surfeit themselves upon it. The larger animals, especially cows and hinds, eat ivy leaves to expel the afterbirth following calving. Foresters also value ivy for this purpose. Ivy further provides a cure for dropsy and constipation.*

Mistletoe (Viscum album) *grows on many New Forest trees, in the copses and in orchards. The Forest gypsies keep their mistletoe gathering places very secret. This plant is powerfully medicinal. Herbalists recognize that the medicine virtues of mistletoe differ with the host tree on which it is parasitical. Mistletoe taken from thorn-trees possesses the most healing virtues. Sheep seek out the fallen foliage of mistletoe, and shepherds think it protects them against the rot. The berries are used in treatment of all nervous ailments, especially hysteria, chorea and epilepsy. Also externally in joint ailments.*

Snow at Hardley

BY SYLVIA OLDROYD

A rare sighting, this,
unlikely as a Dartford warbler;
we hold our breath, watching
as the ripened ice-flower
starts to disseminate
its plumed seeds. They descend
without haste, a flock
of Arctic terns alighting.

Uplifted by this down-drift,
we race upstairs exulting
to gaze covetous
at the whitening field, the thorn
breaking into unseasonal bloom.

Grieg's 'Wedding Day
at Troldhaugen' is on the air;
flakes seem to orchestrate
themselves, a *corps de ballet*
gathering and thinning
to the music's dynamics,
laying a bridal gown over the grass,
netting the spider-veiled eaves,
pelting this joining of sky
and earth with lace confetti

that muffles reality, salves
the rawness of winter's touch,
releases me into my Northern childhood.

But here in the South,
one flurry does not make a blizzard;
no Norwegian white-out prevails
into which we may retreat.
Winter's ephemera drag and dwindle,
defeated by a change of air;
the spread cloth, now threadbare,
fading as a spirit visitation,
longed-for, only half believed-in.

Butts Lawn Christmas Eve

Mrs Willingham Rawnsley lived at Park Hill House, Lyndhurst where her husband ran a school for young gentlemen. In 1904, she wrote a book, *The New Forest,* published by A. & C. Black which treats us to a year-round view of the Forest with each of the twelve chapters representing a month of the year. The book is illustrated with her own watercolours. In the December chapter she describes how, on a sunny, frosty Christmas Eve she is able to sit for an hour to sketch looking down the valley towards Butts Lawn. The resulting painting shows stands of slender, bare-branched birches, green paling on the bank and a single majestic beech. She rejoices in the backdrop of holly, the deep green and scarlet giving variety to the otherwise rather colourless winter hues and also bringing joy indoors as a Christmas decoration.

Squoyling

BY RICHARD REEVES AND GEORGINA BABEY

One of the lesser known hunts that once took place in the New Forest at Christmas time, was the annual squirrel hunt. When this first became a customary expedition is not known, but John Wise writing in 1863, makes mention of the weapons used in the hunting of squirrels. Two types were typically used. The 'squoyle' or 'scale' was a length of wood weighted at one end with a lump of lead and the other type, termed a 'snog', was constructed along the same lines but with the weight being made of wood. The lead type produced a verb 'to squoyle' and gave rise to a local expression where the word squoyle was used when slander was implicated, meaning that something was cast at another. A contemporary account of a hunt appeared in the *Estates Gazette* in 1907.

Squirrel hunting is still carried on 'with more or less cruelty,' it is said, in some of our Crown forests, notably in the New Forest in Hampshire, and it is still the practice to organise squirrel hunts on rather a large scale within the confines of the forest. The great day of the year is December 26 (Boxing Day). The hunters are summoned at an early hour by means of a horn, and the energetic sportsmen sally forth armed with sticks – locally termed 'squoyles', or sometimes 'scoggers' – weighted at the ends with lumps of lead. A cart carrying bread and cheese, and the inevitable beer to put life into the sport, usually accompanies the party. The hunt lasts from daybreak until dusk, when the bag, which usually consists of the dead bodies of 40 or 50 squirrels, is carried to a local inn, where they are made into pies for the squirrel feast.

Gerald Lascelles writing on his retirement, in 1915, from his position of Deputy Surveyor of the New Forest, adds more detail about the weapons, although he confuses the names of the two types. He says of the wholly wooden version, that 'it consists of a stick, about 15 inches long, light, with just a trifle play in it, to the end of which is fixed a round or, better, a slightly pear-shaped ball, about the size of a tennis ball, turned out of some heavy hard-wood.' He makes some interesting observations which may explain where the sport originated, and notes that the weapons never seem to be out of the hand of the local labouring population, 'who can never be induced to put in a week's consecutive honest labour', and that, 'a good deal of "stuff" other than squirrels fall to them'. It seems that the annual squirrel hunt developed out of a need altogether more basic and had probably been carried on for centuries in a less organised manner.

Being a sporting man himself Lascelles did, however, recognise the skill involved in hunting squirrels. He remarks that to see a hunter 'fetch a squirrel out of the tops of the highest branches, sometimes as he bounds from one branch to another, or again as he flattens himself for concealment against the trunk of a tree at ninety feet up, is a perfect revelation'.

The best season for hunting squirrels was the winter when the leaves were off the trees, the great hunts taking place on Boxing Day and New Year's Day. Before the demise of the 'squirrel feasts', which seem to have died out some-time between 1901 and 1907, the Lyndhurst-based gang would return to the Crown Hotel, where the landlord's wife would make the squirrel pie. The end of the feasts may well be related to a severe drop in the squirrel population caused by disease. Some time after the cessation of the First World War, however, squirrel feasts were once again attended; those in Brockenhurst meeting at The Foresters Arms where Mrs Masters, the landlord's wife, would start making the squirrel pie when the gangs returned to the village at lunch time and have the feast ready the same evening.

The responsibility for controlling squirrel hunting lay on Lascelles' shoulders and it is from his correspondence that more information is to be found. In December 1883 one J. Broomfield, a corn factor from Lower High Street, Lyndhurst, wrote to the Office of Woods (precursor to the Forestry Commission) requesting permission to shoot squirrels on Christmas Day. Lascelles, on being asked his views, stated that such licences would be difficult to manage and that Christmas Day was not a suitable day for such an activity. Broomfield's request was refused.

Later, in the autumn of 1902, Lascelles wrote to his superiors on the subject of squirrel hunting in the New Forest. By this time the annual squirrel hunts had grown to such a size that they were causing problems. The hunting gangs were entering the enclosures and 'beating them from end to end' in pursuit of the squirrels and this, in turn, was disturbing all the other wildlife within the enclosures. Lascelles pointed out that even those shooting under licence in the Forest were not allowed within the enclosures and as such they had become important refuges for wildlife.

Lascelles had tried previously to stop such activities within the enclosures, without success, as the gangs involved were too large to tackle with any small force he might be able to muster.

On this occasion he suggested that those involved should be given notice that if hunting was not stopped within the enclosures they would be proceeded against for trespass.

This suggestion was taken up and notices were issued to twenty-six men – the family names of those cited were Broomfield, Browning, Gates, Hull, Phillips, Purse, Rogers, Taplin, Veal, Wiltshire, Whitehorn and Wort – and this seems to have largely solved the problem.

As with all hunting of wild animals there were those who saw the activity as a barbarous assault on a defenceless animal, and a letter to this effect was published in the *Hampshire Independent* in February 1899. No mention is made of the recreational activity and the squirrel numbers recounted seem to suggest that this letter was referring to pest control within the enclosures. However the following year another letter, this time to the *Morning Post* directly refers to the recreational activity in the New Forest. This letter was noted by the Office of Woods staff in the Forest, however they also pointed out that there was significant damage done to trees by squirrels.

In April 1901 the *Hampshire Advertiser* printed letters regarding the recreational hunting of squirrels. The first letter was against the hunting and the other defended the practice. The pro-hunting correspondent suggested that the anti-hunting correspondent should go to the Crown Hotel in Lyndhurst and taste the squirrel pie, after which he would be convinced of the merits of such an activity! Horace Hutchinson stated in his book, *The New Forest*, in 1904, that those who do not eat squirrel when they get the chance, make a great mistake.

The end of the sport did not come about from pressures of the anti-hunting lobby, however, but through lack of the squirrels themselves. In the summer of 1927 questions were asked in parliament as to whether the killing of any more red squirrels should cease in the New Forest 'in view of the increasing scarcity of this interesting little animal'. The reply was to the effect that it would be desirable to maintain a reasonable red squirrel population and 'no more would be killed while the numbers remain low'.

While this seems to have spelled the end of the large organised Christmas gangs the sport was slow to come to an end. Janet Case, a columnist for the *Manchester Guardian* who lived at Hewer's Orchard, Minstead, describes the 'ugly sport' in a diary entry dated 31 December 1928. 'On Boxing Day the boys of the village go out in company in the woods to hunt the squirrel. Their game is to stone them to death. Squirrels are wary and shy and the hunters none too skilful, but they do take their toll of them.'

By 1947, the red squirrel had disappeared altogether. The North American grey squirrel was first seen in the New Forest in January 1940 and soon replaced the native reds. Grey squirrels are more resistant to the diseases which periodically affect red squirrels and when the red population becomes low the greys move into their vacant territories, which the red is then too timid to reclaim. Without doubt the more aggressive grey squirrel has a more detrimental effect on trees and they do not seem in danger of decline.

Gilpin's Picturesque Winter

William Gilpin, well known for his views on the picturesque in nature, was vicar of Boldre for over twenty-six years from 1777 until his death in 1804. When Gilpin came to Boldre his parishioners were an unruly and uneducated band and Gilpin devoted the rest of his life to improving their lot. He built a Poor House and a Model School both of which were the first of their kind in the country. Gilpin wrote many books, mostly topographical, and in 1791 he published *Remarks on Forest Scenery and other Woodland Views (relating chiefly to picturesque beauty), illustrated by the scenes of the New Forest.* This quickly became, and remains, a Forest classic.

Gilpin was also a competent artist and in this extract from his chapter on 'The Seasons', he gives us the benefit of his very definite views on what will make a good winter painting. I wonder if modern artists will agree.

In winter, too, the effect of evergreens is often pleasing. The holly, when it happens to be well combined, and mixed in just proportion, makes an agreeable contrast. The ivy hanging round the oak, if it be not too profuse... is a beautiful appendage to its grandeur.

In a light hoar frost, before the sun and air begin to shake the powder from the trees, the wintry forest is often beautiful, and almost exhibits the effect of tufted foliage. As single objects also, trees, under this circumstance, are curious. The black branches whose under sides are not covered with rime, often make a singular contrast with the whitened spray. Trees also thus covered with hoar frost have sometimes, if not a picturesque, at least an uncommon effect, when they appear against a lurid cloud, especially when the sun shines strongly upon them.

But although many appearances in winter are beautiful and amusing, and some of them even picturesque, yet the judicious painter will rarely introduce them in landscape, because he has choice of more beautiful effects when Nature appears dressed to more advantage.

The painter who chooses a winter subject, in general gives up composition and effect, to shew how naturally he can represent snow or hoar frost. It is almost impossible to produce a good effect with these appendages of winter: they must naturally create false and glaring lights, to which the painter generally makes his composition subservient.

A New Forest Sketch

Philip Klitz was born in Lymington into a great musical family who had emigrated from Prussia around 1790. Klitz moved to Southampton in his early twenties where he became a professor of music and a composer. He loved the New Forest and collected stories, poems and legends of the area. He published a series of these tales entitled *Sketches of Life, Character, and Scenery in the New Forest,* in 1850, five years before his death. It is easy to see why the story of Peter Batt appealed to the musical Klitz. The long sentences, excessive use of semi-colons and 'Americanised' spellings are typical of Klitz's inimitable style.

SKETCHES

OF

LIFE, CHARACTER, AND SCENERY

IN

THE NEW FOREST:

A SERIES OF TALES,
RURAL, DOMESTIC, LEGENDARY, AND HUMOROUS.

———

BY PHILIP KLITZ.

———

LONDON: ORR & CO.   ROMSEY: LORDAN.
1850.

Peter Batt;
or, The Man who lost Christmas-Day

Of all the days in the three hundred and sixty- five, no one was ever so replete with joy and happiness to Peter Batt as the Twenty-fifth of December. With him it had been a red-letter day through life. As a child he frisked and gambolled on his father's hearth; as a youth he had joined in all the gaieties and festivities which that particular period of the year affords; and as a husband and father, Peter had always contrived to indulge, on this day, in the luxuries of the season. For many years he had never failed, by honest and patient industry, to provide hearty and cheerful fare for himself and those dependent on him; and each successive Christmas-day brought with it some new delight or gratification. Truly Peter enjoyed himself to his heart's content, and was never more happy than when surrounded by those he loved; who with their smiling faces warmed and cheered his heart, as they did justice to his kindness and hospitality. Peter was like unto all things human. Honest, simple-hearted Peter had his share of what philosophers (who of course never possess it themselves) call vanity. What! a man living in one of the most retired nooks in the kingdom – a man who had seen and enjoyed upwards of fifty Christmas-days! – the father of six children and husband of Sally Batt, whose tongue might take the pride out of any man – pooh, pooh! Nay, reader, but it was even so! Among the many moral infirmities which poor human nature is heir to, vanity was a besetting fault of poor Peter: but let not the reader labor under the erroneous idea that it was personal vanity on the part of Peter, for here is his picture. From the soles of his feet to the crown of his head, we may fairly estimate a structure of about five feet five, habited with excellent neatness and precision – for it is Christmas-day, and Peter has donned his best. See how brilliantly his shoes glisten beneath the neat black gaiter surmounting them! observe the snowy whiteness of the cotton stockings which enclose his well-proportioned lower limbs, again surmounted by the neat black velveteen con-tinuations. A waggish visitor from the great city once ventured to compare Peter's style of dress to the alternate colours of the magpie; but his witticism failed – Peter stood too high in the estimation of his rural friends to be affected by such observations. Then see the admirable keeping of the picture – how these are relieved by the square homely-cut of his single but straight-breasted snuff-brown coat, with large yellow metal buttons and upright collar! Well, Peter; I see nothing in thee or thy coat whereof an honest Englishman need feel ashamed: thy well-set frame bespeaks thee a man of strength, and doubtless thy sinewy arm and hardened hand have wrought worthily for thee and thine. And then thy good-tempered face, and twinkling grey eyes, whereof one hath a southerly inclination and the other an affection for the north: and withal, thy venerable bald pate. Who shall say thou art not worthy of praise? But where gottest thou that self-satisfied air? Ah! I forget, it is Christmas-day, and thy destiny is to fulfil certain duties, whereof more anon. Say, then, to what conclusion can we arrive as to the cause of our hero's vain glory? Truly he is proud of his six children, and well he may be – for where shall we find four sons and two daughters, in one family, more healthy, or more attentive and dutiful to their parents. Then his wife, his Sally! was there such another housewife in the whole village? To be sure, Sally had a tongue, as well as a will of her own; and sometimes treated honest Peter with what he facetiously called chin-music, but not after the manner of Michael Boai. Yet, take her for all in all, Sally was a good wife, mother, friend, and neighbour; and as Peter

'Was to her faults a little blind,
And to her virtues very kind.'

they jogged on harmoniously together, and enjoyed a very fair proportion of domestic happiness.

But it is necessary, without further prologue, to acquaint the reader with the mainspring of Peter's ambition, and to that end I would direct his observation to that smaller specimen of button which dangles at a little distance from the bright, large, yellow row, that ornaments his snuff-brown coat. On that tiny button 'hangs our tale,' for thereon is wont to depend the object of his devout affection – the rival of mistress Batt in her husband's love – his ever-petted baby – his *bassoon*! Assume, O Reader, inexperienced in the fervent passion which amateur members of the Orphean family often feel for that particular instrument through which (in their own opinion) they 'discourse most eloquent music' – assume, I pray thee, no sceptical air at this assurance, that Peter Batt – worthy man, good husband as he was – did now and then prefer the fellowship of his bassoon to that of Sally – did sometimes find its voice the more enchanting of the two. Did she first learn to love him, I wonder, as with distended cheeks he strove to render his wooden idol lovely in *her* eyes? Madame de Stael somewhere suggests the impossibility of a woman's love being kindled in favor of a man performing on the bassoon; and Sally has therefore an opportunity of acquiring fame by denying (if she is able) the insinuation of the celebrated Frenchwoman.

For forty years, as man and boy, had Peter Batt been a prominent member of our village church choir. He had developed all the varieties to which male voices are subject, and as he was ambitious of reputation, the whole parish had the benefit of his vocal powers. Unfortunately, perhaps, for Peter's future fame as a singer, his father – who was also a bassoon-player – was too much addicted to the habit of flattering his son's 'childish treble,' not hesitating in the boy's presence to declare that Peter had 'a stounden voice,' and that 'ye cou'd hear un down t' bridge' – a distance of nearly half a mile. The natural consequence of this encomium was, that Peter wished to make himself heard *beyond* the bridge, and to that end so shrieked and squalled as ultimately to *crack* his voice irreparably; and notwithstanding all his after efforts, he never could be certain whether the note he were about to sound would prove itself a tenor, counter, or bass note. This was sadly thwarting the aspirant for fame; but when he found that all hope of eminence in that line was quite shut out, he one day, in sheer despair, took down from the bacon-rack (where it had been placed since his father's death), the family bassoon. I should here mention that Peter's common avocation was that of a wheelwright, as his father's had been before him; and I would allude also to a striking historic coincidence, to show why great things might not, under more favorable auspices, have resulted from Peter's cultivation of music. Haydn, the first great symphonist that Germany produced, was the son of a village wheelwright, and his father was also musical: I am not aware, certainly, that he practised the bassoon; but suffice it that he instilled a love of music into his son, who displayed such early genius, and extreme beauty of voice, as to attract the attention of all his friends and neighbours. My readers will recollect the estimation in which the senior Batt held the vocal abilities of his son and heir: doubtless this admiration extended itself generally through the parish, and but for the non-existence of certain national facilities, it is possible that England also might have produced a symphonist. With the music-loving Germans it always formed an integral feature in their system of education; an indispensable requisite in the qualifications of even a village schoolmaster in Germany is a knowledge of music – and here was the advantage which Haydn possessed over our hero, for attracted by the beauty of his voice, we find the singing master of the royal chapel of St Stephen's, in Vienna, visiting the schoolmaster to hear his favorite pupil; the consequence of which was, that Haydn was at once removed to the chapel, where he received a regular musical education; and Germany had the honor of fostering the genius of this illustrious composer. Now, had corresponding advantages been presented in dear Old England, one thing is certain – old Michael Drodge would not have presided over the ploddings of Peter when a student; for poor old Michael in the first place was nearly deaf; in the second, had no knowledge of music, intuitive or acquired; and lastly, held it in supreme contempt, since nature had deprived him of the power of appreciating it. But for these drawbacks is it not *possible* that Peter Batt might have attained celebrity as a composer? (between ourselves, he did make one experiment – with what effect the sequel will show.) But I could not resist this opportunity of remarking on the characteristic differences of the two nations, as it regards music.

Having shown the musical as well as natural origin of our hero, we will now trace him through his earlier years, when, having completed the routine of his education, he commenced his occupation as a wheelwright, under his father. Be it known then that he secured the confidence and esteem of all his neighbours; and that, as the old man's infirmities increased, so did Peter's responsibilities. At length his father died, just as Peter was competent to carry on the business. Behold him now, his own master, with a thriving trade, and no incumbrance – free to make choice of a wife. Under such circumstances, he felt it impossible to resist the influence of his old schoolmaster's daughter, Sally, or rather 'Mistress' Drodge, as she was called by the housekeeper at the manor-house, in which establishment she filled the important situation of lady's maid, and with her smart cap and neat attire, quite unsettled the heart of Peter. I have before stated that he resorted to the bassoon, hopeless of ever becoming a singer; - this was subsequently to his father's death. The fact is, he had been so constant an attendant of the village choir, that he felt quite unhappy in being incapacitated from joining in its performances. This induced him to great exertions, (for he was still ambitious), and he therefore practised whenever an opportunity offered. Could the reader have heard him run up and down the instrument, from the lowest note to the highest, and then close in a cadence of great force and power on the lowest E flat, which he held with a 'stounden' tenacity and tone, he would have been convinced of the strength of his lungs, if not of the purity of his taste. Peter was greatly admired – perhaps rather from the extraordinary loudness of his performance than the delicacy of his expression; but in the particular line he had chosen he could do more than many of the first solo players who have distinguished themselves as bassoonists: he could play the 'College Hornpipe,' 'Country Bumpkin,' or 'Sir Roger de Coverley,' to thirty couples, up and down, in the same evening; and if that is not a pretty good proof of the strength of his lungs, I know not what is. If then 'Music hath charms to soothe the *savage* breast,' and if our hero was thus renowned as one of her most favored votaries, can it be supposed that Sarah Drodge could attend the village church every Sunday, and hear unmoved of the proficiency of Peter Batt? How often did Peter, in the acme of his best achievements direct his angular orbs of vision into the pew that contained the tender object of his passion! To be sure it required some slight acquaintance with Peter's eyes to ascertain their exact direction; but Sarah knew the precise degree of their inclination, and I incline to think – despite the assertions of Madame de Stael – that his inflated cheeks and energetic strains made a deep impression on her heart. To her, Peter Batt, with his bassoon, was a most interesting, if not a romantic specimen of humanity. He had often wished for an opportunity of breathing forth his tender aspirations and vows of eternal love and constancy, when a circumstance occurred that put him at once at rest as to the reciprocity of their feelings.

It had been a custom, from time immemorial, for the choir of the parish church (which respected body of men and boys was under the especial direction of our hero), to perambulate the village during Christmas-eve, singing in and before the houses of the most respectable of the inhabitants, the carols and anthems appropriate to the season: this generally took up a great portion of the night; and at church, on the following day, the same were repeated to the admiration of a very full congregation. Of course this was an 'event' to all the members of the choir in general, and to Peter Batt in particular. On the evening of Christmas-day the choir was always invited up to the manor-house, where the good squire, his family, his visitors, and household, were accustomed to assemble in the hall – some to witness and others to join in the merry-makings which prevailed at this merry period. The performances of the choir were interspersed with the general amusements, which were necessarily suspended for a time, during the business of refreshment; and on one occasion – big with the fate of Mrs Drodge and Peter Batt – by accident or connivance those two personages found themselves seated side by side at the squire's hospitable board. Now was it that Peter felt his waistcoat heave – particularly on the heart's side – with emotions struggling for utterance, which must, alas! continue to struggle, at least till after supper, and then – ! Whether Mrs Drodge's gentle bosom were agitated by sympathetic feelings, I can't affirm so confidently as I could wish; but I still have reasons for thinking that her state of mind was similar to that of a person conscious that a great and long-expected crisis is now close at hand. And so indeed it was. By-and-by it became Peter's turn, in the course of 'blind-buff,' with sealed eyes to pursue – whom, I wonder? For whose accents did he listen with strained ears, and with fixed design – could he but make that capture - to lead his prize beneath the hanging mistletoe, and there -? Did Sally Drodge, with that 'diplomacy' intuitive (as we have before asserted) to lovers – did Sally permit that half-cough to escape, as furnishing a clue to groping Peter, or was it actual necessity which forced that expression? And then, that timid shriek of 'Oh!' as she flies from his extended arms? But still he follows, and she flies not far or fast – and now he grasps her, and bears her boldly under the consecrating Bough, and with unmistakable ardour avails himself of its licence: and I – as her historian – should be sorry to be sworn to say, that Mrs Drodge did her best to elude the pursuit of Peter Batt, or that she resisted his steps towards the mistletoe, or found his salutation so distasteful that its repetition would have angered her. – Our hero was otherwise persuaded, and with reason, since at that very Christmas twelvemonth the village witnessed the nuptials of Peter Batt and Sarah Drodge.

Good reader, as in many a drama of more thrilling interest than the lives and loves of Peter and Sally Batt, it has been the scribe's prerogative to foreclose a tedious current of petty incident, unmarked by any special interest; so now will we imagine an interval of twenty years in the procession of our story, and raise the curtain upon our humble characters after the experience of a score of married years has, let us hope, made Peter Batt a still wiser and better man.

Peter has by this time become an indispensable requisite to the well-being of the village: he has been an honest and industrious man, and has thriven I should think to his heart's content. Sally retains her place in his affections, which has furthermore been strengthened by six additional ties, all promising and healthy. He has extended his business to great advantage – so much so that he has built himself a new house, with workshops and a range of useful out-buildings. And it is a great satisfaction to Peter to stand at some spot which commands the best view of his property, and think that, so to speak, he is 'monarch of all he surveys.' Yet – as no mortal pilgrimage is ever purely bright – the brow of happy Peter was sometimes beclouded with care: even his heart had its vexations – and as his musical genius was instrumental to his discomforts, it will be necessary to make some explanation thereupon.

That 'Woman is fickle' is either a currently-reported fable or a melancholy truism; and though an angel is she in the hour of anguish, yet in the unafflicted moments of her lordly companion doth she too often derive delight in the proof of his subjugation and pleasure in his perplexity. One of Mrs Batt's first demonstrations of displeasure was directed at Peter's much-beloved bassoon, against which, as Mrs Drodge, she had never breathed a syllable to indicate indifference, much less dislike. It was the source of unfeigned consolation to Peter – his bassoon – and she knew it: was she jealous of his having a second bosom-comforter, when the church had put that matter exclusively into her hands? Then, to be sure, he did sacrifice much time to it – time to which Mrs Batt may have thought that holy marriage had entitled *her*, and not 'a plaguey bassoon,' as she was wont in hasty moments to designate that respectable instrument. Now, independently of its conveying a sense of comfort to the ear and breast of Peter, his execution of certain pieces with which his bassoon and his neighbours were become familiar, had long secured the latters' compliments, and had also fired the sons of three of them with the noble zeal of emulation. Could Peter forego with resignation the source of so much pleasure? above all, could he with fortitude relinquish 'the inoffensive manna of soul-sweetening praise?' But Mrs Batt kept up the tune of persecution with wondrous vigor and with weighty argument. 'What,' she would like to know from Peter, 'what would Mrs Cinnamon, the grocer's wife, say of Mr C. if he left her at the church-door on Sundays, to go and join a lot of men and boys? – Would Mrs Sweetbread (the butcher's better-half), allow her husband to 'beneath' himself and treat *her* in such a manner? - She only wanted Peter to speak his mind out, and answer her:' but alas! he, good man, was no match for his wife in volubility, and he therefore dealt with the case

The Sir John Barleycorn where Peter Batt 'assumed considerable boldness.'

in general terms:- 'he wasn't going to *argufy*, nor he wasn't going to put off from playin'.' This was the position which Peter took up at the beginning of the war, and which he stoutly maintained for a time against the sharp-shooting of the enemy; but as in a wordy engagement with wives few men may hope to triumph, so Peter begun at last to shrink from the incessant and raking fire of his spouse; and the result was, that he compromised his dignity as a man to his affection for his instrument, and did, stealthily and away from home, that which he had not courage left to do there. And this was much to be regretted; for upon such occasions Peter was apt to resort to the 'John Barleycorn,' where, privately sore at his humiliation, he would assume considerable boldness –- defy 'th' old 'ooman' (meaning Mrs Batt) – and walk off with a fixed determination to do great things at home in reference to his bassoon, which, however, on arriving there, and yielding to second-thoughts, he was always induced to defer.

Never shone the moon more brightly than on the Christmas-eve of 18—. Never, on any previous occasion, had so much interest been felt as on that auspicious evening, when the good people of the village were surprised in the arms of Morpheus by 'Hark, the herald angels sing!' in original music, composed expressly for the words, by Peter Batt! Yes, Peter had marched forwards; – spite of all opposition and interference, Peter had become a composer. He felt that he was a musician in his heart. We have not space to enter on a critical review of this emanation of his genius, but be assured that all he could do had been done. For some time had he, in kind compliance with Sarah's wishes, forsaken the instrument on which he had been wont to luxuriate; but as the river, when checked, only gathers an increased force, so did his musical genius burst forth in a written composition, which, as it was produced noiselessly and at home, did not excite the observation of his partner. No sooner was it finished than that 'plaguey bassoon' became in constant use; and for six weeks did the choir of the village church, under the superintendence of our hero, practice what he called 'a Christmas Hymn of my own composin'.' It was highly successful, and report soon spread our author's fame. Rival choirs tried to procure copies, but in vain. At length arrived the longed-for night, on which the public were to have their ears regaled with this splendid production. Big with importance, Peter again took up his bassoon, and at the time appointed boldly sallied forth to meet his friends. Before he left his home, a few hints relative to that 'plaguey bassoon' had slightly ruffled his temper; but two or three glasses of punch at the Barleycorn, the rendezvous of the party, dispelled his gloom, and after one trial he felt reassured and animated, and 'was himself again.' At twelve o'clock behold our party issuing forth in the full confidence of meriting the approbation of all those Christians who like to be disturbed from their comfortable slumbers on Christmas-eve. The success of our hero was beyond all precedent – so much gratified were the villagers that many of them rose, protruded their nightcaps, and prayed for it again. The churchwardens had always made a point of having 'something hot' ready for the 'quire' on its arrival at their respective houses. Now both the churchwardens were Peter's particular friends, and a wee drop extra was prepared for him: and with it came that applause so sweet to an author's ears, that our hero, between the cheering cup and acclamations of his friends, positively forgot himself, and by the time the choral party began to wend its way homewards, Peter Batt was in a very elevated and unusual state: – I blush to own it, but Peter was decidedly drunk! Alas

– 'that men should put an enemy
Into their mouths to steal away their brains!'

Thus it was that Peter fell; yes, reader, he fell morally – aye, and he fell physically too; and two men were obliged to support to his home the author of 'A Christmas Hymn of his own composin'.' Behold him – now shouting, then hallooing – now severely remonstrating with a non-present Mrs Batt on her abuse of his bassoon; and now attempting to convince his two supporters of his superiority on that delightful instrument. Totally unconscious of where he was, the poor composer was left at his own door, about six o'clock in the morning. Poor Sarah had gone to bed at the usual hour, in sad despair at this new outbreak; she could not sleep – she was too anxious for her husband to allow of that; she lay listening to their singing until the sound was lost in the distance; and ever and anon she would fancy she heard them returning, and she would leave her bed and look out on the cold, yet bright moonlight, and wish for his return: thus did she pass a restless night, until she saw with pain the state in which he was brought home. She immediately went down stairs, and with immense difficulty contrived to get Peter *up*, and into bed, though perfectly senseless, and overcome with excitement and strong drink. As soon as she had thus disposed of him, she left, to proceed with the numerous duties which devolve on a mother of six children, especially in preparing a seasonable family banquet for Christmas-day: once or twice she took a candle and crept to the room to ascertain if he was still asleep and comfortable. On the third visit she began to perceive that the sun shining through the curtains was unpleasant to him, as he turned round immediately from it. She remedied the difficulty by fastening a blanket doubled across the window to keep out the light; and while she was doing so a scheme occurred to her suddenly which she instantly determined to carry out. There Peter lay, snoring and dreaming, in a condition of sottish clairvoyance: now he fancied the sun was glittering on all nature; and he saw the trees studded, as it were, with myriads of diamonds – the effect of the preceding night's frost; and then he saw his own wife and all the children dressed in their best, hastening away to church; and then they met their neighbours, and the greetings were mutual and satisfactory; and he heard, as he had done for nearly fifty years before, the chime of the village-bells, and he recognised the peal of Christmas-day, and his heart leapt. – But when he tried to jump up and join the pleasant groups he saw, he could not; he had lost all power of motion, and (as he one day confessed to Davy Butler, in confidence,) he 'laid like a thinkin' statty.' Then came another season of thick mist upon his senses, and he fancied that he heard 'the herald angels' singing the hymn 'of his own composin'': then came a volley of applause from listening mortals, which Peter took in greedily – particularly what Davy Butler had said at the churchwarden's, that 'there was nor another such a genus that way as Mr Batt, as *he* cou'd hear on in these'em parts.' Then followed a momentary clearance of the fog which hung upon his faculties, and he lifted his leaden head from the pillow, and peered through the parting curtains into perfect and unrelieved darkness, while all was silent as night. Then again he pillowed his aching head, and in a few minutes another phantasmagoria flitted before his distempered mind: now he thought himself in church, but whereabouts he could not well make out; – there was the good old rector, and there his friend the clerk; there also was the choir – but where was himself, Peter Batt? Straining the socket of his mind's eye in order to discover *that* essential, an indescribable figure now fills and now vacates his place, clutching a huge bassoon: now it rolls backward and forward – now its eyes gleam – now it attempts to carry to its waiting jaw the reed of its bassoon – now after infinite eccentric motions that feat is accomplished, but O! what unearthly noise ensues! – and yes, evidently the bassoonist is drunk, utterly drunk, and in church too! Oh, sin! Oh, shame!

The night appeared long and dreary to Peter, and he looked wistfully towards the window, and longed for some token that it were day: at length his eyes were cheered by the morning-light, peeping in at a corner of the lattice, and Peter bestirred himself to rise. To inspect and remove the strange covering from the window was his first business, and it began to renew in him an uncomfortable state of feeling. Then the appearance of his clothes was horrifying to his sense of propriety, conveying to his mind the idea of Peter Batt – decent and respectable Peter Batt, in shameful prostration of soul and body. Furthermore, a crowning indignity, as penitent Peter felt it, he had now to endure – and he felt too that it must be endured speechlessly – the button had been severed from his coat, by hands in which, morally, he foresaw that he, Peter, must henceforth be mute and passive. His wife, who had been watching his bewilderment, was secretly rejoicing at it, for she foresaw in his confusion and chagrin the perfect success of her scheme. This became the more evident to her when she witnessed Peter's amazement and additional mortification on hearing that he had actually *lost Christmas-day*, and had now awakened on the festival of St Stephen, or the twenty-sixth of December! Reader, my tale is ended. Peter became a more discreet, if not a better man; and I trust many an amateur may learn from his example, that the true source of gratification lies rather in 'the use than in the abuse of art'.

Pemberton Road, Lyndhurst under snow in the late 1970s

'Come to this Forest, when you will,
In Summer bright, or Winter's snow;
You'll not repent the day you came,
But weep the day you go.'

from Gipsies of the New
Forest and other tales,
H. E. J. Gibbins, 1909

Acknowledgements

With grateful thanks to the following:

Peter Roberts, Richard Reeves, Irene Soper, Barry Peckham, Rosemary Manning, Sylvia Oldroyd, David Stagg, Ted Bannister, Stuart Cooke, Desmond A. LePard, Jenni Tubbs, Faber & Faber, Juliette de Baïracli Levy and the New Forest Ninth Centenary Trust Library and Resource Centre.